Holy Spirit,

THE PROMISED ONE

Holy Spirit,

THE PROMISED ONE

LEARNING HOW TO GROW AND
WORK WITH THE HOLY SPIRIT

Frank Bailey

DESTINY IMAGE® PUBLISHERS, INC.

P.O. Box 310, Shippensburg, PA 17257-0310

"Speaking to the Purposes of God for this Generation and for the Generations to Come."

This book and all other Destiny Image, Revival Press, Mercy Place, Fresh Bread, Destiny Image Fiction, and Treasure House books are available at Christian bookstores and distributors worldwide.

For a U.S. bookstore nearest you, call 1-800-722-6774.
For more information on foreign distributors, call 717-532-3040.
Or reach us on the Internet: www.destinyimage.com.

ISBN 10: 0-7684-2509-3
ISBN 13: 978-0-7684-2509-3

Previously published as *Another Helper*, ISBN 1-79451-06-9; Copyright © 1998 by Carpenter's Publishing, New Orleans, Louisiana, USA.

For Worldwide Distribution, Printed in the U.S.A.

1 2 3 4 5 6 7 8 9 10 11 / 09 08 07

Dedication

To my wife, Parris. Your friendship and encouragement on this journey has been beyond words.

Table of Contents

Foreword 9

Introduction 11

Chapter One   Jesus the Savior 13

Chapter Two   The Baptism With the Holy Spirit 27

Chapter Three   Why I Should Speak in
Tongues—Part I 45

Chapter Four   Why I Should Speak in
Tongues—Part II 59

Chapter Five   Why I Should Speak in
Tongues—Part III 69

Chapter Six   Gifts of the Holy Spirit 85

Chapter Seven   The Holy Spirit—The Communicator......107

Chapter Eight   Fellowship of the Holy Spirit....................121

Chapter Nine   Another Helper *(Allos Paracletos)*..............133

Chapter Ten   Jesus and the Holy Spirit: The
                   Purpose of the Anointing 145

Chapter Eleven   The Awesome Trinity 159

Foreword

I am fascinated with the writing of Frank Bailey. *Holy Spirit, The Promised One* is a well-written book for people who have newly found their way into the Kingdom, as well as those who are simply ready for more of God. Through reading this book, believers will soon discover that there is more to their Christian experience than just being born again. Pastor Frank spells out the progressive steps to Christian growth and maturity. He explains that it is possible to be filled with the fullness of God, to enjoy the indwelling presence of the Holy Spirit 24 hours a day, and to watch the Holy Spirit develop in you and activate the gifts of the Spirit in your life.

Holy Spirit,.The Promised One is a book for people who desire to move forward in their Christian experience. Too many people are content to stand still in their walk with the Lord, but this book will help you chart a course for the rest of your life that will bring added blessings to you on a daily basis.

Holy Spirit, The Promised One is easy to understand as well as motivating. I recommend it not only for new converts, but also for people who have been Christians a long time—those who need to be rejuvenated and want to increase the Lord's blessing in their lives.

There is one baptism—an initial experience as recorded in the second chapter of Acts—but there are many fillings. Ephesians 5:18 says that we can be continually filled on a daily basis with the fullness of the Spirit, and this book will help to show you how. I hope that everyone who reads this book will be edified, as I have been.

Dick Mills, Evangelist
Dick Mills Ministries
Orange, California
December 2006

Introduction

"And it shall be in the last days," God says, "that I will pour forth of My Spirit on all mankind; and your sons and your daughters shall prophesy, and your young men shall see visions, and your old men shall dream dreams; even on My bondslaves, both men and women, I will in those days pour forth My Spirit, and they shall prophesy. And I will grant wonders in the sky above and signs on the earth below, blood, and fire, and vapor of smoke" (Acts 2:17-19 NASB).

We live in the beginning stage of what promises to be the greatest spiritual event in history. The Lord has promised a great move of the Holy Spirit in the days before the return of Jesus Christ to the earth. Although spiritual awakenings have happened in various places throughout the history of the Church, there has never yet been an awakening that has shaken the entire earth. But the tide is turning. This is the age and the hour of the ministry of the Holy Spirit. The day of the great out-pouring spoken of by the prophets has begun.

Our relationship with the Holy Spirit is critical in this great outpouring. Every member of the Body of Christ must prepare for this mighty move and learn to rely completely on Him. As we do, great things will begin to take place.

The Holy Spirit is looking for vessels to work through in order to accomplish His mighty plan for our generation. The purpose of this book is to help prepare and equip His people to become those vessels. Surely, as we grow close to Him, His presence will be poured out mightily throughout the earth.

You and I were created to know the Lord intimately. The Holy Spirit brings the Father and the Son into reality in our lives. You were created to know the Father and the Son and to enter into fellowship with Them through the person of the Holy Spirit. As you press on to know the Lord and the Holy Spirit becomes your daily companion, you will experience a deepening of joy and satisfaction in your life. This joy in the Holy Spirit is the joy that Jesus has enjoyed from eternity with the Father. Now, you and I enter into this fellowship and our satisfaction brings glory to the Lord.

As you read this book, I pray that a thirst for the living water that Jesus spoke of would grow in your heart. *"'If anyone thirsts, let him come to Me and drink. He who believes in Me, as the Scripture has said, out of his heart will flow rivers of living water'"* (John 7:37b-38 NKJV).

CHAPTER ONE

Jesus the Savior

My relationship with the Holy Spirit began suddenly and un-expectedly in 1973. I had been raised in a non-Christian home and the turbulent 1960s had taken their toll on my life. Through-out my teenage years and until my early twenties, alcohol and drug abuse had deeply affected my life. I was ensnared by the pleasures of sin and I was lost in a world of darkness. My con-science was telling me that I was living an impure life, but I could not muster the will to change my life. I wanted to do right but I was ensnared by the pleasures of sin.

In August of 1973 my future wife, Parris, and I went to see a movie on Canal Street in New Orleans. The movie was *Jesus Christ Superstar*. The film was a secular telling of the life of Christ. Although there were many errors and contradictions to the Scriptures, there *was* a depiction of the crucifixion at the end of the movie—various artists' depictions of the death of Christ. As I watched this film I became extremely convicted of my lifestyle and found myself weeping and wanting to know this person Jesus for myself.

The movie finished and Parris and I returned to our car weeping and not understanding what was happening in our lives. We went for a drive and found ourselves on the lakefront of Lake Ponchartain. That is where the miracle began to take place.

We heard the sound of singing and the sound of joy in voices that was strangely attractive to us. As we followed the sounds, we came upon some teenage Christians singing to the Lord and sharing their faith.

One of the teens looked into my face and told me words that burned deep within my soul. "Jesus loves you and has a plan for your life." That night Christ came into my heart as I yielded to Him for the first time. I began to taste the reality of God's love and a strange joy that was beyond anything I had ever known. Spiritual transformation was beginning in my soul; old things had passed away and all things had become new. My spiritual journey was just beginning. For the first time the Holy Spirit was becoming a vital part of my life.

The Problem of Sin

All of mankind is born with a problem. We are separated from God. Each one of us is born as part of a fallen race. In the beginning God created man in His image. We were created to walk with Him and to enjoy a fellowship and intimacy unknown to the rest of creation.

And God said, Let Us make man in Our image, after Our likeness: and let them have dominion over the fish of the sea, and over the fowl of the air, and over the cattle, and over all the earth, and over every creeping thing that creepeth upon the earth. So God created man in His own image, in the image of God created He him; male and female created He them (Genesis 1:26-27).

This fellowship with God came to a tragic end. Our first parents disobeyed their heavenly Father, and their lives were deeply affected by their sin.

And the Lord God commanded the man, saying, Of every tree of the garden thou mayest freely eat: But of the tree of knowledge of good and evil, thou shalt not eat of it: for in the day that thou eatest thereof thou shalt surely die (Genesis 2:16-17).

Their fellowship with God was broken and they began to live a life of spiritual darkness, separated from the Lord. The tragedy was even greater because it did not just affect their lives; their future children were affected as well. All of the sons and daughters of Adam and Eve were born with this fallen nature. Even today, every one of us is born separated from God, enslaved to sin, and unable to live a holy life because of these chains of bondage.

Wherefore, as by one man sin entered into the world, and death by sin; and so death passed upon all men, for that all have sinned (Romans 5:12).

Fortunately for us, this is where the grace of God steps in! We were all born in a state of hopelessness, unable to live a godly life, not able to change ourselves.

*And you hath He quickened, who were dead in trespasses
and sins; Wherein in time past ye walked according to the
course of this world, according to the prince of the power of
the air, the spirit that now worketh in the children of disobe-
dience: Among whom also we all had our conversation in
times past in the lusts of our flesh, fulfilling the desires of the
flesh and of the mind; and were by nature the children of
wrath, even as others. But God, who is rich in mercy, for His
great love wherewith He loved us, Even when we were dead
in sins, hath quickened us together with Christ, (by grace ye
are saved;) And hath raised us up together, and made us sit
together in heavenly places in Christ Jesus: That in the ages
to come He might shew the exceeding riches of His grace in
His kindness toward us through Christ Jesus. For by grace
are ye saved through faith; and that not of yourselves: it is
the gift of God: Not of works, lest any man should boast. For
we are His workmanship, created in Christ Jesus unto good
works, which God hath before ordained that we should walk
in them* (Ephesians 2:1-10).

Christ came to destroy the work of sin in our lives. He was
crucified in our place so that we could experience His love
once again. He came and provided the gift of salvation. He offers us salvation by grace through faith, the wonderful gift of
God. This is what I experienced that night on the lakefront of
New Orleans. I did not have the ability to change myself, but
He came. His amazing grace opened my heart to His love.
What I could not do, He did in me. The grace of God inter-
rupted and transformed my life in a moment of time. The
grace of God is our only hope for salvation from the bondage
of our sinful nature.

You Must Be Born Again

There was a man of the Pharisees, named Nicodemus, a ruler of the Jews: The same came to Jesus by night, and said unto Him, Rabbi, we know that Thou art a teacher come from God: for no man can do these miracles that Thou doest, except God be with him. Jesus answered and said unto him, Verily, verily, I say unto thee, Except a man be born again, he cannot see the kingdom of God. Nicodemus saith unto him, How can a man be born when he is old? Can he enter the second time into his mother's womb, and be born? Jesus answered, Verily, verily, I say unto thee, Except a man be born of water and of the Spirit, he cannot enter into the kingdom of God. That which is born of the flesh is flesh; and that which is born of the Spirit is spirit. Marvel not that I said unto thee, Ye must be born again. The wind bloweth where it listeth, and thou hearest the sound thereof, but canst not tell whence it cometh, and whither it goeth: so is every one that is born of the Spirit (John 3:1-8).

How can these things be? How can a man be born when he is old? Jesus taught us that there is only one way to get to Heaven, actually one way to ever see Heaven or heavenly truth at all. He said that we must have a spiritual birth. When our lives are affected by the grace of God, the Holy Spirit actually comes to live inside of us. There is an infusion of the life of God. This is the greatest miracle of all: we are born from above, the life of God in the soul of man. This is what our life is all about. This is why we were born.

This new birth begins to open our eyes. A veil is taken away from our eyes, and we begin to see everything differently. We see our lives differently: our work is different; the Bible is different; Jesus is different; church is different. Everything is changed because we are changed.

This new birth is the beginning of our new life. Until the moment of our new birth we have no way to understand the things of God. Only the Spirit can reveal spiritual truth to us. This infusion of divine life is the only way for us to enjoy spiritual reality.

As Jesus said, "You must be born again."

Drinking Living Water

There is an incredible story in John 4 that describes this new birth experience. Jesus was resting from His travels at a well in the land of Samaria. He began to talk to a woman who was there, asking her for a drink of water. As the woman questioned Him about why He, being a Jew, would even talk to a Samaritan woman, Jesus responded with an incredible statement. *"If you knew the gift of God, and who it is who says to you, 'Give Me a drink,' you would have asked Him, and He would have given you living water"* (John 4:10 NKJV).

He went on to say in John 4:13b-14 (NKJV), *"Whoever drinks of this water will thirst again, but whoever drinks of the water that I shall give him will never thirst. But the water that I shall give him will become in him a fountain of water springing up into everlasting life."*

As the story goes on we find out that this woman had five husbands and was living with a man who was not her husband. This story sounds so familiar. How many people have spent their lives looking for a human relationship to meet the longing need of their soul? This woman is a classic case. All of us search for pleasure to satisfy our thirsty soul. Some search in relationships, illicit sexual affairs, careers, possessions, drugs or alcohol, but all end in the same empty place. Nothing this world offers ever satisfies our thirsty souls. Only the Living Water can satisfy our thirsty souls.

This picture of living water is a glimpse into the reality of salvation. When we are born again, we begin to be aware of the spiritual world. We begin to experience realities that we have never known before. In the tasting of salvation we begin to experience a pleasure far greater and more satisfying than any earthly enjoyment. This joy is the joy of the Lord. This joy is the vehicle that the Lord uses to deliver us from the foolish pleasures of sin.

That night that I accepted Christ on the lakefront, I began to experience the beginning of this joy found only in Christ. This spiritual joy replaced the foolish pleasures of sin in my life. The joy of the Lord liberated my soul from sin and brought me to a place of delighting in God. This is what Jesus meant when He told the woman that if she drank the water He had to give, she would never thirst again. This living water takes away our need to pursue the water of this life. Salvation delivers us from the bondage of sin by attacking sin at its source. The power of sin is pleasure; the pleasures of God destroy our need for the foolish pleasures of this world.

The Righteousness of God

Fallen man does not have the capacity to live a righteous life. Sin is part of his very nature. He has no recourse but to sin. Sin is what he is, so sin is what he does. Jesus was born without sin. The Bible clearly teaches that Jesus was conceived by the Holy Spirit and had a sinless nature. Because of His sinless nature, He lived a sinless life.

Jesus came to this earth to die. He offered Himself as a sacrifice for sin. As a man, He represented mankind when He died on the cross. All of my sinfulness was placed on Christ; my sins were punished, the judgment of God was accomplished, and therefore I am free from the sins of my past.

> *For He hath made Him to be sin for us, who knew no sin; that we might be made the righteousness of God in Him* (2 Corinthians 5:21).

Today when the Father looks at me, all He can see is Jesus. The righteous life that Jesus lived has been credited to me. He took my sin; I received His righteousness. Today I am viewed by God as legally free from sin. There remains, however, a problem. Not only do I need to be viewed as righteous, I need righteousness to be my experience. This again is where the work of the Holy Spirit comes in.

When we are born again, the nature of God is planted within our soul. We live in a fallen world, and still have the effect of this fallen world upon us, but there has been a change. As we fellowship with God through the person of the Holy Spirit, our experience begins to change.

> *For if ye live after the flesh, ye shall die: but if ye through the Spirit do mortify the deeds of the body, ye shall live* (Romans 8:13).

Actually, the more we draw near to God, the more the Spirit takes control of our lives. We begin to experience the practical, experiential side of our salvation by yielding to the Holy Spirit. As we drink of His presence, we are putting to death all of those carnal tendencies in our lives. Salvation begins to run its course in our lives. We are experiencing continual change. As we come under the influence of His Spirit, we are transformed on a daily basis.

> *But we all, with open face beholding as in a glass the glory of the Lord, are changed into the same image from glory to glory, even as by the Spirit of the Lord* (2 Corinthians 3:18).

All Things New

Behold, I make all things new (Revelations 21:5).

The work of salvation is the beautiful work of God. All things are made new in our lives by the Holy Spirit. He makes our hearts new. Before Christ, our hearts were attracted to the things of this world. The fruitless pursuit of sensual satisfaction ensnared all of our hearts. When Jesus comes into our lives, this part of us begins to change. We are suddenly caught by surprise in our love for the things of God.

First, we fall in love with Jesus. Before, He was just a historical figure—He was a good man, a prophet, a religious teacher, but not much more than that. Now He has become altogether lovely to our souls. When we think about His life and ministry, we are stunned and amazed at His love for us, His powerful signs and wonders, and the incredible way He gave His life. Then, we think of Him in His heavenly ministry, and our joy begins to bubble over. He is more than amazing, and He becomes more precious to us every day.

Second, our love for the Word of God becomes brand-new. Before Christ, the Word of God seemed boring and uninteresting to us. Many times we would think about reading it, but distractions would always get in the way. When Christ comes into our lives, all of that changes. God's Word becomes precious and valuable to us. Suddenly, we want to read and study the Scriptures. Our private time with the Lord becomes the highlight of our day. Only God could perform a miracle like that. To hunger after God's Word is one of the great signs of His work of salvation.

Finally, our love for the church is made new. I remember that as a child I despised going to church. Our family rarely went (maybe on Easter Sunday, but not every year), but I hated those times in church. It was so boring to me. All of that changed for me when I was born again. Church became one of the great joys in my life. I could not get enough of singing to the Lord or hearing His Word preached. I looked forward to spending time with all of my new Christian friends. We had something in common. We all loved the same things. Christ had come into our lives and made all things new.

The beginning of our journey into the world of the Holy Spirit begins with salvation. You must be born again. Is Christ in your heart? Have you yielded yourself to God? If not, today is the day of salvation for you. Just become real with God. Ask Him to reveal Himself to you. Salvation is a hungry heart responding to the love of God.

If you are calling out to God, pray a prayer something like this:

Father, I know I am a sinner in need of salvation. Thank You for sending Your Son, Jesus, to die in my place. Father, forgive my sins. Cleanse me now with the blood of Your Son, Jesus. Lord Jesus, I need You. Come into my life and make me new. Thank You for changing my life.

Chapter One
Summary Questions

1. What does it mean to be born again?

2. Why does man need to be born again?

3. How can we be free from sinful pleasures?

4. Why did Jesus have to die?

5. What has the Lord made new in your life?

CHAPTER TWO

The Baptism With the Holy Spirit

We live in an incredible time. Throughout history there have been seasons of outpouring that affected regions of the world. We think of the 18th-century revival that affected Great Britain and North America. We also remember the revival in Wales in the early 1900s and the great Pentecostal outpouring at Azusa Street in Los Angeles in 1906. In our generation we are beginning to experience what, I believe, is the beginning of the last great awakening that will affect all of the earth. Jesus is coming soon and He is pouring out His Spirit on all flesh. He is baptizing hungry people in all nations with the person of the Holy Spirit.

It is the baptism with the Holy Spirit that releases the power to change our world. God is the same yesterday, today and for-ever, and He is going to move again mightily through the power of His Spirit. He wants a people who have a desire inside them that says, "Lord, I want to see Your Spirit move in our city and in our world!"

What Is the Baptism With the Holy Spirit?

The word *baptizo* in the Greek means to be saturated or immersed. The baptism with the Holy Spirit is a saturation or immersion into the Holy Spirit. It is a distinct experience, separate from the new birth. When you accept Jesus Christ as Lord, the Holy Spirit comes to live inside you. He dwells within you. When you are baptized with the Holy Spirit, you are filled to overflowing with the power of God. This is oftentimes known as the infilling of the Holy Spirit or the Holy Spirit coming "upon" you.

The baptism with the Holy Spirit is the empowering of the Holy Spirit as He comes and equips us to live the kind of life that Jesus lived. We receive power, dunamis, to fulfill the Great Commission. Acts 1:8 (NASB) says, *"But you will receive power when the Holy Spirit has come upon you; and you shall be My witnesses both in Jerusalem, and in all Judea and Samaria, and even to the remotest part of the earth."* John the Baptist and Jesus spoke of this baptism in the Gospels as well as in Acts 1:5,8.

The difference between initially receiving the Holy Spirit when you are born again and the baptism with the Holy Spirit is seen in the following Scriptures.

John 20 refers to the day that Jesus rose from the dead, Easter Sunday. This event takes place in the Upper Room, the same place where the disciples were on the day of Pentecost.

Then, the same day at evening, being the first day of the week, when the doors were shut where the disciples were assembled, for fear of the Jews, Jesus came and stood in the midst, and said to them, "Peace be with you." When He had said this, He showed them His hands and His side. Then the disciples were glad when they saw the Lord. So Jesus said to them again, "Peace to you! As the Father has sent Me, I also send you." And when He had said this, He breathed on them, and said to them, "Receive the Holy Spirit" (John 20:19-22 NKJV).

He breathed on the disciples and said, "Receive the Holy Spirit." They received the Spirit of God into their lives, becoming born again of the Spirit, the dwelling place of God Most High. Some 40 days after this, Jesus told them to wait in Jerusalem to receive the baptism with the Holy Spirit.

And, being assembled together with them, commanded them that they should not depart from Jerusalem, but wait for the promise of the Father, which, saith He, ye have heard of Me. For John truly baptized with water; but ye shall be baptized with the Holy Ghost not many days hence (Acts 1:4-5).

John answered, saying unto them all, I indeed baptize you with water; but One mightier than I cometh, the latchet of whose shoes I am not worthy to unloose: He shall baptize you with the Holy Ghost and with fire (Luke 3:16).

Even though the 11 disciples had received the Spirit of God into their lives on that Sunday evening, they were told by Jesus, "There's something else you need: *power* to preach the gospel and touch the world in which you live. Don't leave Jerusalem until the power of the Holy Spirit comes upon you."

The disciples did just that. They "returned to Jerusalem from the mount called Olivet" and entered "the upper room where they were staying" (Acts 1:12-13 NKJV). Acts 2:1-4 describes what took place next, on the day of Pentecost, when the disciples were baptized with the Holy Spirit and fire with the evidence of speaking in other tongues.

> *And when the day of Pentecost was fully come, they were all with one accord in one place. And suddenly there came a sound from heaven as of a rushing mighty wind, and it filled all the house where they were sitting. And there appeared unto them cloven tongues like as of fire, and it sat upon each of them. And they were all filled with the Holy Ghost, and began to speak with other tongues, as the Spirit gave them utterance* (Acts 2:1-4).

So we see in the second chapter of Acts the disciples receiving the baptism with the Holy Spirit as evidenced by speaking in other tongues. In the tenth chapter of Acts, the Gentiles also received the baptism with the Holy Spirit as evidenced by speaking in other tongues.

> *While Peter yet spake these words, the Holy Ghost fell on all them which heard the word. And they of the circumcision which believed were astonished, as many as came with Peter, because that on the Gentiles also was poured out the gift of the Holy Ghost. For they heard them speak with tongues,*

*and magnify God. Then answered Peter, Can any man for-
bid water, that these should not be baptized, which have received the Holy Ghost as well as we?* (Acts 10:44-47).

After we receive the baptism with the Holy Spirit, a new
avenue for God to operate in our lives is opened. A prayer
language is given to us when we "speak in other tongues" as a
means to pray under the guidance of God.

It must be stressed that while the baptism with the Holy
Spirit is evidenced by speaking in other tongues, tongues is
only a part of it. An incredible power source is made available
through the baptism with the Holy Spirit. This power source is
crucial for us as believers in order to change this generation for
God. God wants us to tap into this source as the Church and as
the people of God.

How Important Is the Baptism With the Holy Spirit?

*Then Jesus arrived from Galilee at the Jordan coming to
John, to be baptized by him. But John tried to prevent Him,
saying, "I have need to be baptized by You, and do You come
to me?" But Jesus answering said to him, "Permit it at this
time; for in this way it is fitting for us to fulfill all righteousness." Then he permitted Him. After being baptized, Jesus
came up immediately from the water; and behold, the heavens were opened, and he saw the Spirit of God descending as
a dove, and lighting on Him, and behold a voice out of the
heavens, said, "This is My beloved Son, in whom I am well-
pleased"* (Matthew 3:13-17 NASB).

If you study the ministry and life of Jesus, you will see that the power did not begin until His experience of being baptized with the Holy Spirit. He didn't do miracles as a little boy because He didn't have the anointing of the Holy Spirit yet. He was the last Adam, a man born without sin and born of a virgin. God was indeed His Father and He was the Son of God, but until He received the baptism, He was just like you and me, only without sin.

However, it was when He received something supernatural in Matthew 3:16 that He was clothed with "power from on high" (Luke 24:49) and His miracle ministry was birthed. This power or anointing is what equipped Jesus to minister the last three years before going to be with the Father. Signs and wonders, healings and miracles took place.

If Jesus needed the power of the Holy Spirit upon Him to minister to the sick, how much more do you and I need it? How much more does the Church need it? We need to be endued with God's power flowing out of us to effectively minister to this world.

Who Can Receive the Baptism With the Holy Spirit?

Then they returned to Jerusalem from the mount called Olivet, which is near Jerusalem, a Sabbath day's journey away. When they had entered the city, they went up to the upper room where they were staying; that is, Peter and John and James and Andrew, Philip and Thomas, Bartholomew and Matthew, James the son of Alphaeus, and Simon the Zealot, and Judas the son of James. These all with one mind were continually devoting themselves to prayer, along with the women, and Mary the mother of Jesus, and with His brothers (Acts 1:12-14 NASB).

Acts 1:12-14 is referring to the apostles after Jesus told them to go and wait in Jerusalem for the promise of the Father and not to leave Jerusalem until they received this.

Gathering them together, He commanded them not to leave Jerusalem, but to wait for what the Father had promised, "Which," He said, "you heard from Me; for John baptized with water, but you will be baptized with the Holy Spirit not many days from now" (Acts 1:4-5 NASB).

As we saw in Acts 2:1-4, all who were waiting in the Upper Room received the promise from the Father: the baptism with the Holy Spirit.

Just who were some of the people in this Upper Room when the miracle happened? Simon Peter, Thomas, Mary Magdalene, Mary the mother of Jesus, and many others were up there.

I want you to imagine this. You are a bystander in Jerusalem and you came for the day of Pentecost. You have heard that Simon Peter had been with Jesus. The whole town is in a stir. Jesus has been crucified. There are rumors He had risen from the dead, and Peter supposedly has seen Him.

You see Simon Peter coming down the street and going into the Upper Room. You stop him and ask, "Peter, why are you going to the Upper Room? Why don't you tell me what Jesus has done?" He answers, "I can't right now. I've got to go up into this place, this Upper Room, and receive what the Father has promised. I need to receive what John talked about, this mighty baptism with the Holy Spirit."

There are two ways you can look at Peter. You can look at him as a mighty man of God—because, prior to this time, he had miracles happen when he was with Jesus. He had walked on water as well as other amazing things.

You can also look at him another way, however. He had also done some terrible things. Fifty days prior to this time, the night before Jesus was crucified, he denied the Lord. But now, here was Simon Peter going up to that room.

Imagine what the slave girl who was there when Peter denied the Lord would say if she had watched Peter entering the Upper Room. "Who do you think you are, Peter? Do you think you qualify to receive this mighty power of God? Do you think you qualify to receive the anointing that was on Jesus, the Holy Lamb of God?"

Do you know what Peter could have replied? "I am a new creation in Christ Jesus. All my sins have passed away. I'm going up there to be clothed with power from on high, so I can go into all the world and preach the gospel!"

Thomas was going up there, too. What do you think about him? To this day he has a handle on him: "doubting Thomas." Well, Thomas was there, and he wasn't doubting anymore. He had met Jesus. He had seen the One risen from the dead whose hands and side were pierced. Thomas had fallen to his knees and declared, "My Lord and my God!" He was now going upstairs saying he needed the power of the baptism with the Holy Spirit for God to move in his life to fulfill His promise.

Mary Magdalene, from whom Jesus cast out seven demons, was also in the Upper Room. "Who do you think you are?" (Can't you imagine the Pharisees saying this?) "A woman like you is expecting to get anointed like Rabbi Jesus was? You are a woman of ill repute."

Her response could have been much like Simon Peter's: "I'm a new creation in Christ Jesus. All my sins have been washed away and I've been born again. I've met the Savior, and now I'm going to be clothed with power from on high so that I can go and declare the resurrected Christ with power, signs and wonders following!"

Also present were James and John. You don't see any major problems in their lives. Yes, they wanted to sit at the left and the right hand of Jesus, yet these were men of God who needed to be baptized with the Holy Spirit.

There was someone else in that room: Mary, the mother of Jesus. She was a woman of God and a woman of faith. She had faced ridicule, condemnation, and mockery because she had carried a child in her womb out of wedlock. That was a sin punishable by death in the Jewish culture. The people could have stoned her to death. But what Mary was declaring by her very presence in that room was, "I need to know Jesus not only as my Savior, but also as the Baptizer with the Holy Spirit."

Mary, the mother of Jesus, came out of that room filled with the Holy Spirit, speaking in other tongues. She was declaring, "I may be the mother of Jesus and I may be a woman of faith, but I need a Savior and I need a Lord. I need His power. I need the Holy Spirit in my life."

The people going into that room were normal people. But they came out of that room different! They weren't denying the Lord anymore nor were they ashamed of the gospel. They were baptized with the Holy Spirit and with a fire that burned on the inside and permeated their hearts, catapulting them to go out and proclaim the good news!

The day of Pentecost wasn't the only day when the power of the Holy Spirit operated in their lives. That was just the beginning. If you go through the Book of Acts, you'll find many times where they gathered together and prayed and the Bible says, "They were filled with the Holy Ghost." What resulted was a people who trembled under the power of God, who went out and spoke the Word of God with boldness.

You and I qualify to sit in that room. The Holy Spirit is a free gift to you and me. As long as you have repented of your sins and received Jesus Christ as your Savior and Lord of your life, you can receive the baptism with the Holy Spirit. He is there for the asking. Just receive Him.

Can Anything Hinder You From Receiving the Baptism With the Holy Spirit?

Once again, looking in the Book of Acts, we read, *"These all with one mind were continually devoting themselves to prayer, along with the women, and Mary the mother of Jesus, and with His brothers"* (Acts 1:14 NASB).

I like the first part of that verse where it says *"with one mind"* they were *"devoting themselves to prayer."* In other words, there was no finger-pointing. John and James weren't saying to Peter, "You blew it, Peter. You denied the Lord." No one was pointing a finger at Mary Magdalene saying, "You blew it, Mary. You were outside thinking Jesus hadn't really risen from the dead." No one criticized Thomas when he didn't believe, and Matthew wasn't being reminded by others of all the people from whom he had stolen money. You also don't see anyone pointing fingers at Jesus' brothers who didn't believe in Him until the resurrection. Instead, they were all there, saying and believing the same thing with one accord. There was no complaining or criticizing. Rather, they were praying and seeking God.

What will keep the power from operating and is, in fact, hindering it right now in the Body of Christ? Division, discord, unforgiveness, and bitterness. Harboring unforgiveness in your heart toward someone who has hurt you will keep you from receiving the baptism with the Holy Spirit. However, when you forgive those who have hurt you, you will flow in unity with other brethren, whether you agree with them 100 percent or not.

The Holy Spirit brings us into unity in the Body of Christ. This fellowship that we have with the Father and the Son is the basis of our fellowship with our brothers and sisters in Christ. Our doctrine cannot bring us into unity. Only a heart filled with God can fellowship truly with others.

> *That which was from the beginning, which we have heard, which we have seen with our eyes, which we have looked upon, and our hands have handled, concerning the Word of life – the life was manifested, and we have seen, and bear witness, and declare to you that eternal life which was with the Father and was manifested to us – that which we have*

seen and heard we declare to you, that you also may have fel-
lowship with us; and truly our fellowship is with the Father
and with His Son Jesus Christ. And these things we write to
you that your joy may be full (1 John 1:1-4 NKJV).

As we drink together of the Holy Spirit, we become one. It is experiencing God for ourselves that brings us into true unity. This unity is a display of God's love in our hearts. After all, the Holy Spirit is the Love of God shed abroad in our hearts.

Romans 5:5 (NKJV) says, *"Now hope does not disappoint, be-*
cause the love of God has been poured out in our hearts by the Holy
Spirit who was given to us."

How to Receive the Holy Spirit

In Acts 2:37-38 (NASB), we see Peter addressing the men of Israel regarding the message of Jesus' death and resurrection: *"Now when they heard this, they were pierced to the heart, and said to Peter and the rest of the apostles, 'Brethren, what shall we do?' Peter said to them, 'Repent, and each of you be baptized in the name of Jesus Christ for the forgiveness of your sins; and you will receive the gift of the Holy Spirit.'"*

The first qualification to receive the baptism with the Holy Spirit is **repentance**. Every one of us needs to turn away from our own self-centered ideas, lists, and distractions in the world. You may need to repent of something that isn't necessarily sin but, nonetheless, is a distraction hindering you. Lack of repentance will keep God from pouring out His Spirit in your life.

In Acts 2:33 (NASB), we read the second qualification to receive the baptism with the Holy Spirit: *"Therefore, having been exalted to the right hand of God, and having received from the Father the promise of the Holy Spirit, He has poured forth this which you both see and hear."*

In this passage of Scripture, Peter is talking about the baptism with the Holy Spirit. Jesus received the promise of the Holy Spirit from God the Father. He then poured out His Spirit on those in the Upper Room.

Peter says, "What you have heard and seen are the results of the baptism." There were Jews who were living in Jerusalem at the time who were from every nation in the world. They were amazed because they were hearing their native language being spoken by those in the Upper Room, a room filled with people from Galilee.

The people in the Upper Room were speaking with other tongues as the Spirit of God was poured out upon them. They were speaking in other tongues because Jesus had been seated at the right hand of God the Father and had been glorified. The people in the Upper Room were glorifying Him.

When you repent and turn your back on sin, the only other thing you need to do to receive the baptism with the Holy Spirit is to **glorify Jesus Christ**. Recognize that He has been glorified. He is seated at the right hand of God.

Simply lift your hands and begin to adore Him and worship Him. Worship and praise will bring you directly into the presence of God. Praise God and lift up your voice.

Why don't you do that right now if you have never been baptized with the Holy Spirit?

First, make sure you have accepted Jesus Christ as your Savior. Now pray and ask the Lord to fill you with His Holy Spirit. Lift your hands and begin to worship God out loud. Say whatever comes to your mind. It could be something like, "Lord, I love and praise You. I glorify and honor You. I worship You, Jesus."

Luke 11:13 tells us that it is God's desire to give you the Holy Spirit: *"If ye then, being evil, know how to give good gifts unto your children: how much more shall your heavenly Father give the Holy Spirit to them that ask Him?"*

Once again we look at Acts 2:14-19 (NASB):

> *But Peter, taking his stand with the eleven, raised his voice and declared to them: "Men of Judea, and all you who live in Jerusalem, let this be known to you and give heed to my words. For these men are not drunk, as you suppose, for it is only the third hour of the day; but this is what was spoken of through the prophet Joel: 'And it shall be in the last days,' God says, 'that I will pour forth of My Spirit on all mankind; and your sons and your daughters shall prophesy, and your young men shall see visions, and your old men shall dream dreams; even on my bondslaves, both men and women, I will in those days pour forth of My Spirit and they shall prophesy. And I will grant wonders in the sky above, and signs on the earth below, blood, and fire, and vapor of smoke.'"*

We are experiencing today the beginning of the fulfillment of Joel's prophecy. God is pouring out His Spirit on all flesh. We must yield to His outpourings and not resist Him. The more we embrace His presence, the hungrier we become. The more we drink His living water, the more we want. We must join together with the Holy Spirit and say, "Come, all who are thirsty, and drink. Drink this water and you will be satisfied with God."

I believe that there are degrees of His Anointing. What we have experienced is great, but there is so much more of Him that He wants to pour out. Our hearts are crying out for worldwide revival. We say, "More, Lord. More of You and less of me. More of Your glory. Let the whole earth be filled with the glory of the Lord!"

Chapter Two

Summary Questions

1. What does the Greek word *baptizo* mean?

2. What did Jesus say would happen after the disciples were baptized with the Holy Spirit?

3. What experience birthed the ministry of Jesus?

4. There are two qualifications listed in this chapter to receive the baptism with the Holy Spirit. What are they?

CHAPTER THREE

Why I Should Speak in Tongues — Part I

On the day of Pentecost we see a very unusual gift initiated. As the disciples began to experience the outpouring of God's presence, they all found themselves speaking in an unusual language. They were speaking languages unknown to themselves as they yielded to the power of God being poured out. Some were speaking in languages understood by some of the crowd that was rapidly gathering.

We do hear them speak in our tongues the wonderful works of God (Acts 2:11).

The Lord is still pouring out this very unusual, precious gift. The natural man can sometimes be ashamed of the supernatural demonstrations of God. Some try to minimize the importance of our prayer language, treating it as insignificant and something to be hidden away in some back room. I believe that this is a very serious mistake and robs the Church of its supernatural heritage. We desperately need the power of God in this generation. Praying in tongues is the doorway into this supernatural realm. In these next few chapters we will look closely at the precious gift of the supernatural prayer language. Maybe today will be the day that you receive this gift for the first time, or perhaps it will be deepened in your life.

Starting here and continuing through the following chapters, we are going to look at 16 reasons why every believer should speak in tongues.

◆ **The first reason every believer should speak in tongues is because tongues are a restoration of divine communication with God.**

First Corinthians 14:2 (NASB) says, *"For one who speaks in a tongue does not speak to men but to God; for no one understands, but in his spirit he speaks mysteries."*

When man was first created, he had something wonderful that he unfortunately lost in the garden of Eden: a tremendous fellowship with God. He could walk with God in the cool of the day and he could talk to Him as a friend, face to face. But Adam and Eve fell out of fellowship with God and a wall of separation was built. That divine communication between man and God was shut down. However, when you are born again, your spirit is made alive in Him. When you are baptized with the Holy Spirit, you are given the ability to communicate with God. You receive a prayer language and the lines of communication between you and God are opened. Divine communication is restored.

Let's examine this more closely. First Corinthians 14:2 (NKJV), *"He who speaks in a tongue does not speak to men but to God."* There is a time when the gift of tongues is given in the church for the purpose of interpretation, when God is speaking to us. Someone will come forth with a tongue and either he, or someone else, will come forth with an interpretation. This is a message from God to us. But notice in this passage of Scripture it says, *"He who speaks in a tongue does not speak to men but to God."* This is a type of tongue where God is not speaking to me — as in the gift of tongues and interpretation — but rather, I am speaking to God.

First Corinthians 14:14 (NKJV) says, *"For if I pray in a tongue, my spirit prays."* This means that it is not my mind praying, but my spirit. The time when you are praying in tongues and your spirit is praying, rather than your mind, is important because our minds, our own natural thoughts, are one of our biggest problems in communicating with God. Our thoughts separate us from the thoughts and plans of God.

When you pray in tongues, however, your spirit prays God's thoughts and God's plans. When you are praying in tongues, you are plugged into God and expressing yourself to Him out of the deep, deep recesses of your spirit.

First Corinthians 14:15 (NASB) reminds us not to ignore our natural language, however: *"What is the outcome then? I will pray with the spirit and I will pray with the mind also; I will sing with the spirit and I will sing with the mind also."*

Both your prayer language and natural language are vital in communicating with God. As we spend time praying in our heavenly language, we become more aware of the spiritual realm. Every day we spend a large amount of time doing just natural things, but when we begin to yield to the Lord and pray in the Spirit, the things of earth grow dim and the heavenly world comes alive to us. Jesus becomes real to us; the heavenly Father becomes real to us. We begin to experience the intimacy that we were created to enjoy. This enjoyment of the heavenly world becomes stronger and stronger as we grow in the things of the Spirit. Pray with the Spirit and with your understanding and enjoy this restoration of intimacy with God.

◆ **The second reason every believer should speak in tongues is that tongues joins us together and makes us walk in unity and fellowship.**

But you, beloved, building yourselves up on your most holy faith, praying in the Holy Spirit, keep yourselves in the love of God, waiting anxiously for the mercy of our Lord Jesus Christ to eternal life (Jude 1:20-21 NASB).

In the eleventh chapter of the Book of Genesis, you will see a very unusual event that took place. The natural mind wants to make you think it didn't really happen, or that it might have only been a fairy tale or some type of symbolic story. But in Genesis chapter 11, we read about a people on the earth who were building a great tower, the Tower of Babel. The people were building it as a monument unto the greatness of man, a monument unto themselves.

Let's read the account:

*Now the whole earth used the same language and the same words. ...They said to one another... "Come, **let us build for ourselves a city, and a tower** whose top will reach into heaven, and **let us make for ourselves a name**...."*
*The Lord came down to see the city and the tower which the sons of men had built. The Lord said, "Behold, they are one people, and they all have the same language. And this is what they began to do, and now **nothing which they purpose to do will be impossible for them**. Come, let Us go down and there confuse their language, so that they will not understand one another's speech." So the Lord scattered them abroad from there over the face of the whole earth; and they stopped building the city. Therefore its name was called Babel, because there the Lord confused the language of the whole earth...* (Genesis 11:1,4-9 NASB).

The people were flowing together to glorify themselves. The Bible says God looked down and saw that they were leaving Him out. It appeared that they were going to be able to complete the tower, and if they stayed unified, nothing would have been impossible for them.

Then God came down and confused their language. As a result, they could no longer communicate with each other and were no longer unified. Therefore they took their different languages and separated throughout the face of the earth. It was the beginning of the dispersion of humans all across the world.

But notice that what took place at Babel was reversed on the day of Pentecost. Acts 1:14 and 2:1 state that on the day of Pentecost, "they were all together in one accord." This was just like Babel, only on Pentecost they were to-gether to glorify the name of Jesus and not a man or the name of man.

The people in that Upper Room on the day of Pentecost came together with one accord. They were all filled with the Holy Spirit, speaking in other tongues. People from all different nations of the earth were there. Rather than hearing confusion, they heard God being glorified in their own languages. A great restoration took place on the day of Pentecost. Not only was there a restoration of man's fellowship with God, but man was being restored with man, coming together with man to walk in unity under the name of Jesus.

Read Jude 1 verses 20-21 (NASB) again, keeping in mind this restoration of unity, man with man, and man with God: *"But you, beloved, building yourselves up on your most holy faith, praying in the Holy Spirit, keep yourselves in the love of God...."*

The Bible says we are to flow together with one mind, one heart, one accord and one purpose. As we pray in the Spirit, the love of God is poured out and released in our lives. This incredible, supernatural love is the source of unity in the Body of Christ. Keep yourself in the love of God, praying in the Holy Spirit. When you pray to-gether, something happens in the Spirit that knits your hearts together in love by the power of the Holy Spirit and by the love of God.

◆ **The third reason we should speak in tongues is to build ourselves up on our most holy faith.**

But you, beloved, building yourselves up on your most holy faith, praying in the Holy Spirit (Jude 1:20 NASB).

Faith is the supernatural ability given to us by the Spirit of God to perceive the things of the Spirit. Just as we have the five senses in the natural world — taste, hearing, sight, touch, and smell — we have spiritual senses as well. The ability to experience the spiritual realm was destroyed at the fall of man; however, this ability to perceive God was restored by the cross and the outpouring of the Spirit. We take advantage of this benefit as we yield to the Spirit and pray in tongues.

As we spend times praying in the Holy Ghost, our faith is strengthened. Our awareness of God becomes stronger. We hear His voice when we read the Word. We see His glory displayed in His creation. We feel His presence falling upon us. This is the realm of faith.

Brothers and sisters, build yourselves up in the most holy faith praying in the Holy Ghost. We live in a dangerous world, riddled with unbelief. Our protection from this un-belief is the tangible presence of God. As we pray in tongues, our faith is strengthened, and we begin to hear His voice, see His glory, and feel the touch of His hand upon our lives.

◆ **The fourth reason everyone should speak in tongues is that tongues edify us.**

One who speaks in a tongue edifies himself...(1 Corinthians 14:4 NASB).

Edifying yourself means to bring yourself into the awareness of God's presence.

There is a phrase that was used years ago during the Pentecostal outpouring in the early 1900s. It is found in some Pentecostal churches even now; however, we haven't seen it used too much in the charismatic movement. The phrase is "praying through."

The first time I heard this phrase was a number of years ago at a Pentecostal ministers' conference. When I arrived at the conference, I saw people doing something I had never seen before when it came to worshiping God. My wife, Parris, and I were used to an atmosphere where worshiping God was a wonderful time. We would sing, dance, and shout with other believers who were as joyful as we were. But here, everyone appeared very sad. They were crying and pulling their handkerchiefs out. For a minute, I thought I'd come into a place where something terrible must have happened!

Then I realized what was going on. Every time these people came together they thought they had to repent. They also thought that if they didn't have a strong crying session, the service wasn't really good. When their crying spell was over, things would be fine for the week, but the next week they would go through the same process all over again.

The phrase they used when they did this was called "praying through." What that phrase actually means is "praying in the Spirit," or praying in tongues, until you become aware of the presence of God. These precious Pentecostal brethren had misunderstood the terminology of previous generations. They thought that praying through was just repentance, but didn't understand that repentance was only the beginning. Praying through was actually praying until God's glory fell down. When His glory comes, the prayer meeting really begins.

God doesn't go anywhere and He doesn't change. His glory fills the earth always and He is here right now. What we have to do is bring ourselves into an awareness of His presence by praying in tongues.

You need to get out of the physical or natural mind, which wants to rule and control your life. Praying in the spirit edifies us, stripping away the natural and bringing us into an awareness of God's presence.

If you're not doing that every day in your life, you're not going to know what it means to walk in the Spirit. You will walk in the natural man, still saved, but leaning on the arm of the flesh, rather than depending on the Holy Spirit. This results in a frustrating Christian experience. There is really no difference in your day-to-day lifestyle than that of the world except for the fact that you are going to Heaven. That's a good difference, and it's a big difference, but there's more to Christianity than that.

God wants us to walk in the Spirit and live a Spirit-empowered, Spirit-energized life. That never happens until you pray yourself consciously into the presence of God every day.

Holy Spirit, THE PROMISED ONE

◆ **The fifth reason every believer should speak in tongues is that God will come on the scene and help see you through any weakness you may be fighting. He will bring you to victory in that area through the power of His Spirit.**

Romans 8:26-28 (NASB) is a powerful passage about praying in tongues.

In the same way the Spirit also helps our weakness; for we do know how to pray as we should, but the Spirit Himself intercedes for us with groanings too deep for words; [one translation says "which cannot be uttered in articulate speech"] *and He who searches the hearts knows what the mind of the Spirit is, because He intercedes for the saints according to the will of God. And we know that God causes all things to work together for good to those who love God, to those who are called according to His purpose.*

Those verses are talking about praying in tongues. The first part of verse 26 says, *"Likewise the Spirit also helps in our weaknesses"* (NKJV).

In the Greek there are a number of words joined together to make one word, *sunantilambanomai*, which is translated in English as "helps in our weaknesses" (NKJV) or "helps our weakness" (NASB). Simply translated, *sunantilambanomai* means "help us." However, the more complete definition in Strong's Greek Dictionary is "to take hold of opposite together; to cooperate, assist, help."

The Holy Spirit grabs hold with you, pulling against something that's pulling against you. God grabs hold of

54

you through the person of the Holy Spirit and pulls with you against a weakness that you have.

If you are having a trial, or are tempted to fall into sin in some area of your life, seek help from the Holy Spirit. You recognize the sin or the temptation and say, "Lord, I have a problem with this area in my life and I need Your help. Holy Spirit, You're the Helper. Please begin to help me right now to overcome this temptation." Then the Holy Spirit will help you overcome the problem. Pray in the Spirit and He will help you.

I have a hard time when people with certain habits tell me they just can't quit. *Yes, you can!* You can quit any habit with the help of the Holy Spirit. Your willpower might be weak, but the Holy Spirit is strong and He will join together with you against any habit or weakness that you have.

Cigarette smoking is reportedly as addictive and hard to kick as using heroin or cocaine. I know it is an area in which many say they simply can't quit. But the facts are, the Holy Spirit is stronger than nicotine. He is also stronger than alcohol. These bondages are psychological, physical, and spiritual and they can bind you and make you a slave if you don't draw from the strength of the Holy Spirit. The power of the Holy Spirit is greater than any of those chains of bondage!

Spend time daily speaking in tongues and in centering your understanding on Him. God will come on the scene and begin to help you against any weakness. He will pull with you.

Chapter Three

Summary Questions

1. What was lost in the fall of man that is restored through our prayer language?

2. What role does the prayer language play in walking in unity?

3. What is the connection between faith and the prayer language?

4. How does our edification and spiritual growth relate to the prayer language?

5. What role does our prayer language have in the Holy Spirit's ministry of helping us?

CHAPTER FOUR

Why I Should Speak in Tongues — Part II

◆ One of the great ministries of the Holy Spirit is the ministry of intercession. This brings us to **the sixth reason we should pray in tongues: Many times we do not know how to pray for ourselves. When we pray in tongues, many times we are praying over our own lives the supernatural prayers of God.**

Romans 8:26 (NASB) says, *"In the same way the Spirit also helps our weakness; for we do not know how to pray as we should, but the Spirit Himself intercedes for us with groanings too deep for words."* When you pray in tongues you can pray for yourself. In fact, praying for yourself is something extremely important that you should do every day. Not only do you need to worship God, pray for others, and bring your requests before the Lord, but you need to pray over yourself because you will face struggles, temptations, and challenges in this life.

There are many things you don't know how to "pray for as you ought," as the Bible says. Situations such as what faces you tomorrow or an attack from the devil which you can't see are areas only the Holy Spirit knows. When you pray over yourself, the Holy Spirit prays for and with you over these areas.

Pray in your understanding for the things you know about and pray in the Spirit for the things you don't know about. Paul said, *"I will pray with the spirit and I will pray with the mind also…"* (1 Cor. 14:15 NASB).

When I pray for myself, I will begin by praying in tongues for an extended time.

Many times I will begin to get impressions about things going on in my life. I will then begin to pray with my natural language. In this way the Holy Spirit will lead me supernaturally in intercession over myself.

◆ **The seventh reason every one of us needs to pray in tongues is that when we pray in the Spirit, we pray for others.**

And He who searches the hearts knows what the mind of the Spirit is, because He intercedes for the saints according to the will of God (Romans 8:27 NASB).

This says the Holy Spirit is praying for the saints according to the will of God. The word "saints" in the Scripture is not referring just to Peter, Mary, James and Joseph, who to some are the only saints. It's not referring to the New Orleans football team either! But it is referring to every true believer in the Body of Christ. The Holy Spirit prays for the saints—the true believers—when you and I pray in tongues.

The Lord has chosen to work through human vessels. He preaches through humans and He prays through humans. One of our greatest honors is to be a coworker with the Holy Spirit. He knows all things and knows the plans that He has for the world. As we pray in tongues, He prays through us the purposes and plans that He has for others. This is a tremendous display of God's love shed abroad in our hearts. As we pray in tongues, God's love is focused toward those we are praying for. We have no idea the struggles and challenges others are going through, but He knows. What a blessing it is to be God's instrument of love focused on the needs of others!

◆ **The eighth reason we should pray in tongues is that tongues help us pray according to God's will.**

The last part of Romans 8:27 says, *"according to the will of God."* God makes intercession for the saints according to His will.

One of the awesome blessings connected to our prayer language is praying the will of God. For us, the future is a great mystery. We have hopes and expectations for our future, but the plans of God are locked up until He chooses to display His plans and purposes. There are incredible blessings and incredible challenges ahead of us all.

Part of praying the will of God is connected to yielding our own will, which will come into conflict with God's plans for our lives. As we pray in the Spirit, there is a yielding of our heart. As we yield, the Holy Spirit begins to change us so that we can actually enjoy His coming plans.

There is also a work of preparation being done. He equips us with the necessary tools for the challenges that are ahead of us. The anointing is the equipment we need for the challenging days ahead.

♦ **The ninth reason every believer should pray in tongues is that when you pray in the Spirit, you will see that God is working all things together for His plan to those who are praying according to His will.**

And we know that God causes all things to work together for good to those who love God, to those who are called according to His purpose (Romans 8:28 NASB).

What an awesome passage of Scripture! The Lord is working everything out in my life according to His plan. In verses 26 and 27 of Romans 8, Paul talks about supernatural prayer. The Lord actually anoints us to pray the will of God. The all-knowing God orchestrates events on the earth through our prayers. The Lord searches to and fro throughout the earth to find a heart turned toward Him. When He finds this heart, this person, He anoints them to pray. As we yield ourselves to the Lord, praying in the Spirit, we begin to pray the will of God. The Lord answers these prayers and orchestrates the events of our lives for our good. How incredible are the ways of the

Lord! He plans the events of our lives and brings them to pass by anointing us to pray supernatural prayers according to the will of God. He is causing all things to work together for the good in our lives. What an awesome God!

◆ **The tenth reason we should speak in tongues is that praying in tongues plugs us into the wisdom of God.**

But just as it is written, "Things which eye has not seen and ear has not heard, and which have not entered the heart of man, all that God has prepared for those who love Him." For to us God revealed them through the Spirit; for the Spirit searches all things, even the depths of God. For who among men knows the thoughts of a man except the spirit of the man which is in him? Even so the thoughts of God no one knows except the Spirit of God. Now we have received, not the spirit of the world, but the Spirit who is from God, so that we may know the things freely given to us by God, which things we also speak, not in words taught by human wisdom, but in those taught by the Spirit, combining spiritual thoughts with spiritual words (1 Corinthians 2:9-13 NASB).

Man has limited knowledge, but our Lord is all-knowing. He begins to give us glimpses into His plans as we pray in the Spirit. As we press into God, we begin to have bits of His wisdom unveiled to us. He begins to show us the *"deep things"* of the Spirit (1 Corinthians 2:10 NKJV).

Verse 10 tells us that we can know what God is going to do: *"God has revealed them"* (1 Cor. 2:10 NKJV). "Them" refers to the things God has prepared for those who love Him. These things are revealed to us through His Spirit. They are no longer mysteries. He reveals things to us by

His Spirit: *"For the Spirit searches all things, yes, the deep things of God. For what man knows the things of a man except the spirit of the man which is in him? Even so no one knows the things of God except the Spirit of God"* (1 Cor. 2:10b-11 NKJV).

The Spirit of God within you knows your innermost thoughts and being. He *"searches all things...the deep things of God."* By praying in the Spirit, He begins to reveal or unfold God's wisdom to you.

When you pray in tongues you are not praying with your natural mind but from your spirit. Your mind doesn't understand what you are praying. Tongues allow you to tap into the wisdom and mind of God because the Spirit of God knows the *"deep things of God."*

The mysteries of this great universe are known by the Spirit of God. He knows what is happening across the globe. He knows the plan He has personally ordained for your life and my life. A revival lies ahead of us, and He also has that clearly in focus!

God doesn't want to keep these things a mystery hidden from you. He's not playing hide and seek with His will, His plans, and His wisdom to those who seek His face continually.

If you pray in tongues and seek Him and read the Word, God will drop an idea into your heart. If you will follow through on that idea, you will find it will be exactly the right thing at the right place at the right time. You will be plugged into the wisdom of God. This helps us in our family, ministry or business realm because we become people with legal, insider, privileged information.

In the last few years there were several men and women who were arrested for insider trading because they were on the inside of certain deals they manipulated to profit themselves. You and I also have access to inside information; however, this information is not illegal and will work in every area.

Perhaps your struggle is a practical one. You may need to know how to deal with a teenage child who's not walking the way he's supposed to. You have done all you can and you don't know what else to do. If you start praying in tongues and bring that child before the Lord, God will give you insight into his life and give you direction for how to deal with him. God's wisdom will be breathed into your heart, and you will respond and relate to your child in the best way possible in order to be effective.

God imparts to us His wisdom, His plans, steps and ideas when we pray in the Spirit.

Chapter Four

Summary Questions

1. What role does the prayer language have in inter-
    cession?

2. What role does the prayer language have in pray-
    ing according to God's will?

3. What role does praying in tongues have concern-
    ing turning bad situations around?

4. What is the relationship between wisdom and the
    prayer language?

CHAPTER FIVE

Why I Should Speak in Tongues — Part III

As we continue to look at why every believer should speak in tongues, First Corinthians 14:21-22 (NASB) gives us the eleventh reason:

> *In the Law it is written, "By men of strange tongues and by the lips of strangers I will speak to this people, and even so they will not listen to Me," says the Lord. So then tongues are for a sign, not to those who believe but to unbelievers; but prophecy is for a sign, not to unbelievers but to those who believe.*

◆ **The eleventh reason everyone should speak in tongues is that tongues is a sign for the non-Christian world.**

If you travel around the world today, you will find great churches being built for God and thousands of people coming to Christ. In city after city across America, the largest churches in the world are Spirit-filled, full-gospel churches. For example, the largest church in the world is Yoido Full Gospel Church in Seoul, South Korea. One main factor you will find at Yoido Church is that the people there pray in tongues fervently! Multiple thousands of Spirit-filled believers lift their voices at the same time and worship God in tongues.

The largest churches in Asia, Japan, and Africa today are full-gospel, Spirit-filled churches, as are the largest churches in Latin and South America. The reason these churches are experiencing unprecedented growth is because God's power is being released as these believers pray in tongues. When the power of the Holy Spirit is released, people are drawn to Christ. The non-Christian world recognizes God's power.

In Acts chapter 2 we see the first time people in the Bible prayed in tongues as they gathered together in the Upper Room. The people on the streets heard them and some were hearing their native languages being spoken. Acts 2:11 (NASB) says, *"Cretans and Arabs — we hear them in our own tongues speaking of the mighty deeds of God."* Peter responds in Acts 2:15-16 (NASB): *"For these men are not drunk, as you suppose, for it is only the third hour of the day* [or nine o'clock in the morning]; *but this is what was spoken of through the prophet Joel."*

These non-Christians on the street were in essence asking, "What does this supernatural utterance mean?" Peter explains the baptism with the Holy Spirit to them. That day 3,000 people were born again. We see clearly in this passage of Scripture that praying in tongues drew the people to Christ. God was evident there. His presence is evident when we pray in the Holy Spirit.

The world is looking for a supernatural experience. Over the last couple of decades, people have been interested in Ouija boards and fortune-telling. More and more, individuals have looked to psychics and to the occult, longing for the supernatural that they are not finding in many of their churches. People are tired of dead churches that have a form of godliness, yet are devoid of power. They want to experience God. When we pray in the Holy Spirit, we pray a supernatural utterance from God. Our mind is not praying, but our spirit, energized by the Holy Spirit, is praying. This makes Christians and non-Christians alike aware of the presence of God. It is one of God's advertising tools.

What a tragedy it is to invite someone to a prayer group or a church service and hope the people praying in tongues don't pray too loudly, or that prophecy doesn't come forth because of the fear that the person visiting might not accept God. The underlying thought is, "I hope there is no supernatural manifestation. I hope God is not here today. If God shows up, this person might not accept Him." But realize, brothers and sisters, that praying in tongues is God praying! The Holy Spirit is praying through you in a supernatural utterance, and others will be drawn to Christ because they will sense God's presence there! How vital is our prayer language! It is an outreach to the lost.

The last portion of Isaiah 28:11-12 (NASB) tells us another reason God gave us our prayer language: *"Indeed, He will speak to this people through stammering lips and a foreign tongue, He who said to them, 'Here is rest, give rest to the weary,' and, 'Here is repose,' but they would not listen."* This is a prophecy written 700 years before Christ. It is a prophecy the apostle Paul quoted in First Corinthians 14:21 regarding our prayer language. Paul quotes Isaiah saying that God was going to speak to the world through the prayer language. Through this supernatural utterance many people would be brought to salvation.

◆ **The twelfth reason we should speak in tongues is that praying in tongues is therapeutic.**

It's the therapeutic medicine of God! Our physical minds do not have all the answers. If you are experiencing stress, worry, and anxiety over a particular situation, you need to pray in tongues in order to enter into God's therapy for your life. Therapeutic prayer brings rest, refreshing and peace to your soul.

The world looks to other things for therapy. It looks, for example, to exercise. Many people spend long periods of time exercising to vent their frustrations, hoping to enter into some sort of rest or peace. You can run four miles and enter into peace, but you enter into exhaustion at the same time! You can eat nothing but health food to try to purge your system from impurities and poisons and think this will provide the peace you are looking for. Or you can try to satisfy yourself by overeating! You can even drink until you become intoxicated, obtaining a temporary peace, only to find that when you awaken, your problems are still there. The peace you found is false, and nothing has changed.

The Bible says that when we pray in tongues, we enter into God's refreshing and rest. We're casting our problems, worries, and doubts on Him. We lift our hands and worship Him saying, "God, I don't understand, but I'm trusting You that You're going to work out everything. I worship You, Lord God. I worship and praise You." God then begins to refresh you, not from your mind, but from your spirit. That is where the peace comes from!

Psychiatrists and therapists can deal with the mind, but they cannot deal with the spirit of man. They don't know how. God deals with the root of the problem, which is the inner man. When you begin to pray in tongues, you will find that you can rest in God.

◆ **The thirteenth reason we should all speak in tongues is that tongues bring God's anointing on the scene and that anointing breaks the devil's power.**

Isaiah 10:27 says, *"And it shall come to pass in that day, that his burden shall be taken away from off thy shoulder, and his yoke from off thy neck, and the yoke shall be destroyed because of the anointing."* Isaiah is prophesying about the king of Assyria as well as the devil's yoke on our shoulders. He says, *"...and the yoke shall be destroyed because of the anointing."* This is saying that the anointing of the Holy Spirit breaks the yoke of oppression off of our lives.

The anointing of the Holy Spirit brings freedom. There are demonic entities in this world that oppress, discourage and afflict us with sickness, poverty, confusion and strife. But this passage of Scripture says that the *anointing* of the Holy Spirit *breaks* that oppression, or yoke, or whatever it might be that is trying to hold us in bondage.

In the Book of Joshua, the children of Israel possessed the land of their promises. They attacked city after city and, with God's help, they were victorious in their battles. These cities and pagan civilizations were involved in various sorts of witchcraft and idolatry in the land of Canaan. These cities are like the oppression that exists in the world today. The whole world, without Christ, lies under the influence of the oppression to control people's lives. We have an anointing from the Holy One. This anointing is released when we pray in the Spirit. The enemy is no match for the greater One who lives in us and comes to the scene when we pray in tongues.

The devil has been given too much credit for far too long. He is no match for the Lord. The glory of God comes on the scene when we worship the Lord. Let God arise and let His enemies be scattered.

"Not by might nor by power, but by My Spirit," says the Lord of hosts (Zechariah 4:6 NASB).

Ephesians 6:14-17 (NASB) shows us the armor that God has given us for our protection:

Stand firm therefore, having girded your loins with truth, and having put on the breastplate of righteousness, and having shod your feet with the preparation of the gospel of peace; in addition to all, taking up the shield of faith with which you will be able to extinguish all the flaming arrows of the evil one. And take the helmet of salvation, and the sword of the Spirit, which is the Word of God.

All of this armor is defensive in purpose except the sword of the Spirit, which is offensive. The sword of the Spirit is the Word of God. The Greek word translated as "Word" here is the *rhema* Word of God, or the words that are spoken out of our mouths. Many of us have always applied this "sword of the Spirit, which is the Word of God" to Scripture verses being quoted over our lives; however, that is only half of the power of the sword of the Spirit. When you pray in tongues, the Holy Spirit is praying. It isn't you, but the Spirit of God who is in you. If it is the Holy Spirit praying, then the words of the tongues being prayed are God's words. When we apply the sword of the Spirit through our prayer language, God's words are being spoken right out of our mouths!

After referring to the sword of the Spirit in Ephesians 6:17, the next verse says, *"With all prayer and petition pray at all times in the Spirit..."* (Eph. 6:18 NASB). When we take the Word of God and combine it with our prayer language, we tear down strongholds. I am convinced that the more we pray in the Holy Spirit, the more His anointing will bring liberty and deliverance into our lives. When He brings liberty and deliverance into our lives, He brings liberty and deliverance to the people we influence. Ultimately, as we join together in the power of corporate prayer, princes and principalities that have held us, as well as our cities, in bondage will be pulled down. God's anointing will be poured out, *breaking* oppression and demonic strongholds, as we pray *God's* words through our prayer language.

◆ **The fourteenth reason we should speak in tongues is that tongues open the door into the supernatural world of God.**

In Acts 3:7-8 (NASB), we see the first healing miracle after Christ's death and resurrection. A lame man had been in the temple for 38 years until this point when he met with Peter: *"And seizing him by the right hand, he raised him up; and immediately his feet and his ankles were strengthened. With a leap, he stood upright and began to walk; and he entered the temple with them, walking and leaping and praising God."*

There is an invisible spiritual world in which you and I were created to function. God is Spirit. We are spirit beings, as we were created by God in His image. When we are baptized with the Holy Spirit, a new door to the world of the supernatural opens for us. It is a world that God inhabits, and that man was created to inhabit. Strongholds are torn down in this world, and authority is given to us by God in this world, so that we can live victoriously on earth. Learning to function in awareness of the spirit world becomes normal to the Christian who prays in tongues.

In Acts 3:7-8, Peter began to live in this world. He was launching out into the realm of the supernatural. We see this supernatural world throughout the Book of Acts. A man was healed in Acts chapter 3. In Acts chapter 5, multitudes are healed. The Church began to expand and grow throughout the Book of Acts, as people were praying in tongues and launching out into the supernatural.

God wants you to live in His supernatural world! He wants you to live victoriously, dwelling with Him. Spend extended periods of time praying in the Holy Spirit and enter the supernatural realm that God inhabits. You may not have a disciplined prayer life. Make a decision today to schedule time with the Lord daily. Begin to launch out into the spiritual world praying in other tongues. For too long Christians have been afraid of the spiritual world, yet our prayer language brings us into this new realm, the realm of the Holy Spirit, where we can easily defeat satan.

◆ **The fifteenth reason we should all speak in tongues is that Jesus' prayers are being released through us when we pray in the Holy Spirit.**

Romans 8:34 (NASB) says, *"Who is the one who condemns?* [referring to the devil] *Christ Jesus is He who died, yes, rather who was raised, who is at the right hand of God, who also intercedes for us."*

Jesus is seated at the right hand of God making intercession for the Church. When I think of this passage of Scripture, I always remember what Jesus told Peter the night He was betrayed. In Luke 22:31-32, He said:

And the Lord said, Simon, Simon, behold satan hath desired to have you, that he may sift you as wheat: But I have prayed for thee, that thy faith fail not: and when thou art converted, strengthen thy brethren.

Jesus said something in the midst of that statement that stuck with Peter. It was also recorded in the Gospels. Jesus said, "Peter, I've prayed for you. After you're converted...." In other words, after you are turned around, Peter.

How did Jesus know Peter would turn around? Because He had prayed for him. I have confidence in the prayer of the Lord Jesus Christ! Don't you? His prayers will be answered! Here's the key to Jesus' prayers being answered. Prayer by design has to be uttered on earth. Man was placed on this earth and given delegated authority. He lost that authority when he fell into sin. But Jesus came and gained it back.

Matthew 28:18 (NASB) says, *"And Jesus came up and spoke to them saying, 'All authority has been given to Me in heaven and on earth.'"* Jesus gained all authority when He was raised from the dead and ascended into Heaven. When we pray the Word of God, and when we pray in the Holy Spirit, Jesus' prayers are being released on earth. Jesus is interceding for your next door neighbor through your prayer language. He is praying for that person to get saved. He has determined to work through us to influence our world. As Jesus prays before the Father, the Holy Spirit anoints His children on earth to pray. What an incredible privilege it is to be coworkers with God to see His prayers fulfilled on earth!

Start praying in tongues for your family and your neighbors. Just think, God is praying for them through you.

His will, when we pray in the Holy Spirit and Jesus' words, will be released on earth in His mighty name.

◆ **The sixteenth reason we all should speak in tongues has to do with our tongue itself. Speaking in other tongues helps us enjoy the benefit of a controlled tongue.**

James tells us of these benefits.

For we all stumble in many ways. If anyone does not stumble in what he says, he is a perfect man, able to bridle the whole body as well. Now if we put the bits into the horses' mouths so that they will obey us, we direct their entire body as well. Look at the ships also, though they are so great and are driven by strong winds, are still directed by a very small rudder wherever the inclination of the pilot desires. So also the tongue is a small part of the body… (James 3:2-5 NASB).

James 3:2-5 compares the human tongue to a bit that we put into a horse's mouth to control its body and a rudder that steers a ship, directing the course of its destiny. The tongue directs our lives, but it also bridles our bodies. The tongue affects the human body. There is a connection between our tongue and our brain, and between our tongue and our nervous system. Brain surgeons and neurologists have identified a connection between what is said and the signals that the brain sends to the rest of the nervous system.

The Bible says that the tongue bridles the body. When we begin to pray in the Holy Spirit, we are yielding our tongue totally to God. We are not in control of it anymore, saying what we want to say or what our minds have conceived. Rather, we are saying what the Holy

Spirit is saying through us. Our tongue is totally yielded to God. God is then able to bridle our bodies. It is as if He gets on the horse and begins to ride. *He* then directs our lives in the paths they should go.

A wild horse doesn't accomplish much, b*ut a horse that has been trained and bridled can go out and do great exploits!* When you pray in the Holy Spirit, you bridle yourself. God is able to take hold of the reins of your life and bridle your body. The blessing is: He brings *life* and *healing* to your body. He brings soundness to your mind and *discipline* to your life! He obtains control of your life because the tongue is the key to the control of your life.

Think about how someone is saved. He confesses with his mouth that Jesus is Lord, and believes in his heart that God raised Him from the dead (see Rom. 10:9-10). We have to say it, "I accept Jesus Christ as my personal Lord and Savior. Jesus, You are my Lord." We yield our tongue and praise God in the Holy Spirit, constantly turning over the lordship to Jesus Christ. Praying in the Holy Spirit is saying, "Lord, ride me, direct me, steer the course of my life."

And God wants to! He wants to bless you with all that He has for you. He can do that when you yield your tongue — your life — to Him!

Take these 16 truths on why every believer should speak in tongues and utilize them. Spend extended time in prayer with your heavenly Father. If you don't have a prayer life yet, start where you are. Pray for 5 minutes, 15 minutes, 30 minutes, and eventually pray for an hour. Pray in the Holy Spirit and watch how you will experience God's prosperity and blessing in your life!

Chapter Five
Summary Questions

1. What effect does speaking in tongues have on the unbelievers?

2. What role does the prayer language have in dealing with stress?

3. How does the prayer language affect demon spirits?

4. What relationship does the prayer language have to the realm of the Spirit?

CHAPTER SIX

Gifts of the Holy Spirit

Now concerning spiritual gifts, brethren, I do not want you to be unaware. You know that when you were pagans, you were led astray to the mute idols, however you were led. Therefore I make known to you that no one speaking by the Spirit of God says, "Jesus is accused"; and no one can say, "Jesus is Lord," except by the Holy Spirit. Now there are varieties of gifts, but the same Spirit. And there are varieties of ministries, and the same Lord. There are varieties of effects, but the same God who works all things in all persons. But to each one is given the manifestation of the Spirit for the common good. For to one is given the word of wisdom through the Spirit, and to another the word of knowledge according to the same Spirit; to another faith by the same Spirit, and to another gifts of healing by the one Spirit, and to another the effecting of miracles, and to another prophecy, and to another the distinguishing of spirits, to another various kinds of tongues, and to another the interpretation of tongues. But one and the same Spirit works all these things, distributing to each one individually just as He wills (1 Corinthians 12:1-11 NASB).

All Spirit-baptized Christians have been given the gifts of the Holy Spirit. First Corinthians 12:11 clearly says that God divides the gifts among the Body of Christ and we are to be used in these gifts. First Corinthians 12:7 says that the gifts have been given to us to profit the Body of Christ.

Out of the nine gifts of the Holy Spirit, God may use two or three in our lives more regularly than the others. Usually, one or more of the gifts will be more predominant than the others. They may also not work exactly the same way in each individual. But God can choose to operate any of the gifts at any time, as He wills. First Corinthians 12:3 says that one of the tests of the spiritual gifts is to be certain it honors and lifts up the name of Jesus.

The nine gifts can be divided into three categories:

1. Revelation

2. Power

3. Inspiration (vocal)

Revelation (Reveal)	Power (Do)	Inspiration (Say)
Word of Wisdom	Gift of Faith	Prophecy
Word of Knowledge	Working of Miracles	Gift of Tongues
Discerning of Spirits	Gift of Healing	Interpretation of Tongues

The easiest way to remember these three is that *revelation* gifts *reveal* something, *power* gifts *do* something, and *inspiration* gifts *say* something.

The word of wisdom and word of knowledge, for example, reveal something about a person or a situation. Notice also the phrase, "word of knowledge." It isn't complete knowledge, but a word of knowledge or a bit of knowledge. The same applies to the "word of wisdom." It isn't total wisdom, but a bit of wisdom. Discerning of spirits is also a gift that reveals something.

We should remember not to be dogmatic and concerned with identifying the gift every time it is in operation and say, "That is a gift of...." However, it is important to know the gifts and have an understanding of how they work.

Many times the gifts are like a chain and they work in conjunction with each other. Often, the word of knowledge will be contained within the gift of prophecy. Or, the working of miracles may be released through the supernatural gift of faith. The gift of healing can come directly as a result of a word of knowledge. The important thing is that the gift is being released and is in operation, and not whether it is defined as a word of knowledge or a gift of prophecy.

Revelation Gifts (Reveal)

♦ **The word of wisdom** — supernatural revelation of the divine purposes of God in Christ communicated to the Church through a believer. This gift unveils in part the purposes of God on earth.

♦ **The word of knowledge** — when God reveals to a believer something that now exists or did exist on earth.

- **Discerning of spirits**—insight into the spirit world, whether good or bad. Discerning of spirits is not necessarily always dealing with demons. It can be in the realm of angels or discerning people's spirits as well. It is the ability to see the presence or activity of a spirit. As with the first two revelation gifts, discerning of spirits works in different ways from time to time.

All these gifts are supernaturally imparted. You cannot receive the information from a book. The word of knowledge is a bit of information that you ordinarily would have no way of knowing, except that God supernaturally gave it to you. The word of wisdom is a piece of information concerning God's purposes.

Power Gifts (Do)

- **The gift of faith**—supernatural revelation of the unseen world. The ability given by God to sense the world of the Spirit. This world becomes real to us by the power of the Holy Spirit.

- **Working of miracles**—the supernatural intervention by God in the ordinary course of nature. In this gift, God works through a person or through some instrument.

- **Gift of healing**—a special gift given by God to heal various sicknesses.

Inspiration Gifts (Say)

- **Prophecy**—a supernatural message given to edify, exhort, and comfort, with the emphasis again being on the supernatural. Anyone can say something edifying or comforting, or remember a Scripture, but the emphasis here is that prophecy is a supernatural word of God.

◆ **Gift of tongues** — a message from God in a spirit language to the Body for the purpose of interpretation. There is a difference between the gift of tongues for the purpose of interpretation and our prayer language. We all have the ability to pray in tongues. When we do, we are speaking to God and not to man (see Chapters 3, 4, and 5). But when God speaks to us, He moves on an individual using the gift of tongues, and that person receives a message from God in a spirit language to the Body. The interpretation should follow either through the same person or someone else.

◆ **Interpretation of tongues** — interpretation, not translation, of an utterance from God.

Revelation Gifts

Word of Wisdom

The word of wisdom is considered by most people to be the most important and highly esteemed of the gifts. Remember from the definition that it has to do with the future plans and purposes of God. Many times what we call *prophecy* is really the word of wisdom in operation. Old Testament prophets prophesy, speaking an oracle regarding the purpose of God. God spoke to me in 1978 and said, "Frank, I want you to build a church in the city of New Orleans. I want you to build a church that's going to affect every neighborhood and every part of the community. I'm going to pour out My Spirit." That was a word of wisdom as to the purposes of God for the city of New Orleans.

Word of Knowledge

A word of knowledge reveals to a believer something that now exists or did exist on earth. Say, for example, you are walking down the street and see a man at the corner store. You are moved in your spirit to share with him that everything is going to be okay. His wife is going to come back if he will just give his life to Jesus Christ. That is a word of knowledge. A man was waiting there for you to come and give him a message. Acts 9:10-12 (NASB) also shows us a word of knowledge in operation:

> *Now there was a disciple at Damascus named Ananias; and the Lord said to him in a vision, "Ananias." And he said, "Here am I, Lord." And the Lord said to him, "Get up and go to the street called Straight, and inquire at the house of Judas for a man from Tarsus named Saul, for he is praying, and he has seen in a vision a man named Ananias come in and lay his hands on him, so that he might regain his sight."*

This is a word of knowledge. Ananias received a specific bit of information that he otherwise had no way of knowing. It was divinely revealed to him that a particular man was in a certain place. That man's name was Saul, who is also known as the apostle Paul. The Lord told Ananias to go and put his hands on Saul so that Saul might receive his sight. Immediately prior, Saul had met Jesus on the Damascus road and was temporarily blinded. He went to Damascus to a particular house and waited and prayed. The Lord spoke to Ananias and sent him to where Saul was waiting. Ananias received a word of knowledge, or a supernatural bit of information. The Holy Spirit spoke to him in a vision.

In Acts 9:13-16 (NASB) we see the word of wisdom in operation:

> *But Ananias answered, "Lord, I have heard from many about this man, how much harm he did to Your saints at Jerusalem; and here he has authority from the chief priests to bind all who call on Your name." But the Lord said to him, "Go, for he is a chosen instrument of Mine, to bear My name before the Gentiles and kings and the sons of Israel; for I will show him how much he must suffer for My name's sake."*

God was giving Ananias a bit of information about His purposes. God's purpose was to raise Saul up as an apostle and bring the message of the gospel to the non-Jewish world. Prior to that time, Christianity was basically a Jewish religion. Some non-Jewish people had been saved, but it was the exception rather than the rule. But now Paul was going to take the message to the Gentile world. Today the Body of Christ is 99.9 percent Gentiles. So, we see a word of knowledge and then a word of wisdom being used to reach out and minister to the apostle Paul.

Matthew 24:3-9 (NASB) shows us another example of the word of wisdom:

> *As He was sitting on the Mount of Olives, the disciples came to Him privately, saying, "Tell us, when will these things happen, and what will be the sign of Your coming, and of the end of the age?" And Jesus answered and said to them, "See to it that no one misleads you. For many will come in My name..."* [Jesus is beginning to operate in the word of wisdom], *"...saying, 'I am the Christ,' and will mislead many. You will be hearing of wars and rumors of wars. See that you are not frightened, for those things must take place, but that is not yet the end. For nation will rise against nation, and kingdom against kingdom, and in various places there will be famines and earthquakes. But all*

*these things are merely the beginning of birth pangs. Then
they will deliver you to tribulation, and will kill you, and
you will be hated by all nations because of My name."*

In this entire chapter, Jesus is beginning to receive bits of information from the Father concerning His future. He didn't have an entire panorama of everything that was going to happen in the last days. Even Jesus said that the time of His coming no man knew, not even the Son, but only the Father in Heaven. But He received hints of information, words of wisdom from God about the future. He distributed some of that information to the Church.

You see the same gift in operation in the Old Testament. Isaiah 53 and Psalm 22 are glimpses into Christ's future suffering on the Cross.

Let's look at an example of a word of knowledge in Jesus' ministry.

*And Nathanael said to him, "Can any good thing come out
of Nazareth?" Philip said to him, "Come and see." Jesus saw
Nathanael coming to Him, and said of him, "Behold, an Israelite indeed, in whom there is no deceit!" Nathanael said
to Him, "How do You know me?" Jesus answered and said
to him, "Before Philip called you, when you were under the
fig tree, I saw you." Nathanael answered Him, "Rabbi, You
are the Son of God; You are the King of Israel." Jesus answered and said to him, "Because I said to you that I saw
you under the fig tree, do you believe? You will see greater
things than these" (John 1:46-50 NASB).*

Jesus had a word of knowledge. He knew Nathanael was sitting under a fig tree. He told Nathanael that bit of information as God gave it to Him, and it caused Nathanael to take notice and see that Jesus was the Christ, and he began to follow Jesus. Jesus simply used one little bit of information, one word of knowledge, to reach into Nathanael's heart.

Another example of Jesus operating in the word of knowledge is in John 4:15-24 (NASB):

> *The woman said to Him, "Sir, give me this water, so I will not be thirsty nor come all the way here to draw." He said to her, "Go, call your husband and come here." The woman answered and said, "I have no husband." Jesus said to her, "You have correctly said, 'I have no husband'; for you have had five husbands, and the one whom you now have is not your husband; this you have said truly." The woman said to Him, "Sir, I perceive that You are a prophet. Our fathers worshiped in this mountain, and you people say that in Jerusalem is the place where men ought to worship." Jesus said to her, "Woman, believe Me, an hour is coming when neither in this mountain nor in Jerusalem will you worship the Father. You worship what you do not know; we worship what we know, for salvation is from the Jews. But an hour is coming, and now is, when the true worshipers will worship the Father in spirit and truth; for such people the Father seeks to be His worshipers. God is spirit, and those who worship Him must worship in spirit and truth."*

Jesus told the woman that she had had five husbands and that the man she was currently living with was not even her husband! How did Jesus know that? He wasn't going around as God. He gave up His rights as God. He was a man. God gave Him that bit of information to use in order to reach into the woman's heart.

Second Kings 6:8-12 (NASB) shows us an Old Testament example:

> *Now the king of Aram was warring against Israel; and he counseled with his servants saying, "In such and such a place shall be my camp." The man of God sent word to the king of Israel saying, "Beware that you do not pass this place, for the Arameans are coming down there." The king of Israel sent to the place about which the man of God had told him; thus he warned, so that he guarded himself there, more than once or twice. Now the heart of the king of Aram was enraged over this thing; and he called his servants and said to them, "Will you tell me which of us is for the king of Israel?" One of his servants said, "No, my lord, O king; but Elisha, the prophet who is in Israel, tells the king of Israel the words that you speak in your bedroom."*

Elisha was receiving words of knowledge concerning the plans of the Syrian army. He was telling the Israelite king about the Syrians' plans, spoiling all the Syrians' plans and attacks. Elisha was so accurate in what he told the Israelite king that the Syrian king thought he had a spy in his camp. It was actually God giving Elisha inside information, a word of knowledge into the Syrian army's plans.

Think of a businessman operating in these gifts, whom God has raised up to create finances for the Kingdom of God. If his heart totally belongs to God, it could be incredible. Just imagine: "Drill over here and you will strike oil!" God is not going to do that for someone who simply wants to obtain wealth for himself, someone who is self-centered. But if you truly have a heart centered on God, He will give you a word of knowledge, a new idea to earn finances for the Kingdom of God.

God wants us to be at the right place at the right time. He can use the word of knowledge in so many different ways. Think of all the possibilities. We think of it in getting people healed and saved. And that's very good. However, there are many more opportunities when God can use His words of knowledge, as He did in reaching out to the woman at the well.

Discerning of Spirits

Second Kings 6:14-18 (NASB) shows us an example of discerning of spirits:

> *He sent horses and chariots and a great army there, and they came by night and surrounded the city. Now when the attendant of the man of God had risen early and gone out, behold, an army with horses and chariots was circling the city. And his servant said to him, "Alas, my master! What shall we do?" So he answered, "Do not fear, for those who are with us are more than those who are with them." Then Elisha prayed and said, "O, Lord, I pray, open his eyes that he may see." And the Lord opened the servant's eyes, and he saw; and behold, the mountain was full of horses and chariots of fire all around Elisha. When they came down to him, Elisha prayed to the Lord and said, "Strike this people with blindness, I pray." So He struck them with blindness according to the word of Elisha.*

The Syrian king sent an army to capture Elisha because Elisha was telling the Israelite king the Syrians' strategies. Elisha's servant saw the Syrian army and became afraid. But notice Elisha's response: *"Do not fear, for those who are with us are more than those who are with them."* Then after Elisha prayed for his servant's eyes to be opened so he could see into the supernatural realm, the Lord allowed the servant to see that the *"mountain was full of horses and chariots of fire all around Elisha."*

Sometimes the discerning of spirits is being able to literally see spirits with your spiritual eye. Seeing angels appearing, for example, is the operation of the discerning of spirits. Actually, seeing the spirits is one operation of discerning of spirits, but not the only one. Just because you do not see something does not mean that you're not discerning spirits in other ways. One way discerning of spirits works is through God actually giving you a glimpse into the supernatural realm for just a moment. It could be to see angels or it could be to see demon spirits. God might give you a glimpse into the supernatural realm and see a demon that's oppressing someone. Or you could see a demon trying to come against and destroy an individual, church, or region.

Discerning of spirits many times can also be the ability to look into the intentions and motives of a person's heart. Jesus knew the heart of men. It is very important for us to be able to do this. Love and hate, for example, can easily be discerned. Often you can go into a room and pick up on the atmosphere of what has been taking place. If you sense that something is not right, maybe there has just been an argument. You are picking up on what has been going on in people's hearts and in their spirits. When someone comes into the ministry or the business world, you must be able to look into his heart. There are many con artists out there. You must be able to discern in order to protect your interests and the interests of God's Kingdom.

I remember one incident that took place when I was first beginning my ministry. A well-known and respected pastor had a guest come to New Orleans to share with all the pastors in our area how to build our churches and generate more finances.

Both the host and the guest were well-respected pastors, and the guest pastored one of the largest churches in the country.

Unfortunately, the presentation turned out to be a multi-level marketing program! Now, I do not have a problem with multi-level marketing programs. They are a great way to make money. But I refuse to use position and the relationships of the church to obtain wealth. It's wrong! I had to look into this person's motives. He wasn't concerned about us and our money. He wanted to build his pyramid and get rich. He was using the gospel to make money.

You would be shocked at the people who come to us and want to use their multi-level marketing program in our cell system. Multi-level marketing programs are fine, but you cannot use ministry for that. We must be able to look into the hearts of men and sense the purpose of their lives. God protects us with that gift.

Jesus knew Judas' heart using the discerning of spirits, as we see in John 6:70 (NASB): *"Jesus answered them, 'Did I Myself not choose you, the twelve, and yet one of you is a devil?'"*

He recognized that Judas was not all there. The Father had shown Him. I believe there was a time when Jesus selected Judas believing that he was going to be a man of God. He looked into his life and saw potential. Something changed in Judas' life, however, and verse 70 doesn't really say when, where, why or how. It does say in John 12:6, however, that Judas was stealing money from the treasury of the ministry. He began pilfering the Lord's money at some point in time, and Jesus knew about it. We know that Jesus knew about it simply because the event was recorded in the Bible. Here Jesus is beginning to say that He is fully aware of the situation and uses the discerning of spirits to see what was taking place.

Power Gifts

Gift of Faith

The gift of faith is a very special faith, distributed by the Holy Spirit for special times to accomplish special feats. Normal faith is supernatural. It is the opening of our hearts to the unseen spiritual world. All of us were lost walking in darkness. The day Jesus came into our lives all of that changed. In a moment of time we became aware of the unseen world. Faith is the awakening of our spiritual senses to perceive the realms of God.

The gift of faith is similar but even stronger. The Holy Spirit distributes a specific gift of faith in unusual times, many times in moments of crisis. This burst of faith releases an ability to perform or receive supernatural intervention into our world.

Daniel 6 shows another example of the gift of faith in operation. As Daniel was being thrown into the lion's den, he was full of peace. Daniel, Shadrach, Meshach,and Abednego were operating in the gift of faith. They received unusual faith for an unusual moment in time. If we walk with God, God can and will release unusual faith for unusual exploits.

Think of Jesus the night in Gethsemane when He was praying, *"...My Father, if it is possible, let this cup pass from Me..."* (Matthew 26:39 NASB). What a struggle He was going through that night! "God, if there is any other way to go through this… Please let there be some other way." *"…yet not as I will, but as You will"* (Matt. 26:39 NASB). He gave over His will. Something changed inside. I believe the gift of faith began to operate. It would take faith for Jesus to go and lay Himself down on the cross. He didn't go struggling, squirming and kicking. Rather, He went as a sheep led to the slaughter. He went and laid His life down by faith, knowing He was going to be raised from the dead. The gift of faith gave Him the assurance of His resurrection. So, Jesus needed a gift of faith. He didn't need just the normal faith to get by from day to day, but supernatural faith to go to Calvary knowing He would be raised up from the dead.

Working of Miracles

Jesus turned the water into wine in John 2:7-9. He multiplied the loaves and the fish in John 6:11, and walked on the water to save His disciples in John 6:19. These are all examples of working of miracles. First Samuel 17:34-36 (NASB) in the Old Testament shows us another:

> *But David said to Saul, "Your servant was tending his father's sheep. When a lion or a bear came and took a lamb from the flock, I went out after him and attacked him, and rescued it from his mouth; and when he rose up against me, I seized him by his beard and struck him and killed him. Your servant has killed both the lion and the bear; and this uncircumcised Philistine will be like one of them, since he has taunted the armies of the living God."*

What David did to the lion, the bear, and the Philistine was not the result of his being a great slingshot shooter! It was something supernatural. We think that he practiced for hours with his sling and became an expert marksman, but that is not what happened. He did not attack that lion with his bare hands because he had been pumping iron. It was the working of a miracle.

We see a similar manifestation in the life of Samson. Samson's strength came not because of physical power but by the anointing of the Holy Spirit. The anointing would come upon Samson and miracles would take place. He ripped a lion in two with his hands, defeated 1,000 Philistines with the jawbone of a donkey, and even brought down a temple to Dagon by the power of the Holy Spirit. The working of miracles included physical power as seen in the examples of David and Samson. But God can operate in the working of miracles in any number of ways.

Gift of Healing

A page cannot be turned in the four Gospels without seeing the gift of healing in operation. Everywhere Jesus went He healed the sick.

> *And a leper came to Him and bowed down before Him, and said, "Lord, if You are willing, You can make me clean." Jesus stretched out His hand and touched him, saying, "I am willing; be cleansed." And immediately his leprosy was cleansed* (Matthew 8:2-3 NASB).

> *When Jesus came into Peter's home, He saw his mother-in-law lying sick in bed with a fever. He touched her hand, and the fever left her; and she got up and waited on Him. When evening came, they brought to Him many who were demon-possessed; and He cast out the spirits with a word, and healed all who were ill* (Matthew 8:14-16 NASB).

Healing is a demonstration of the love of God. This gift was seen continually in the ministry of Jesus. As He was moved with compassion, He healed the sick.

One of my favorite stories in the Bible is the healing of the woman with the issue of blood. This poor woman had been miserable for 12 long years. One day, Jesus was passing nearby. She pressed through the crowd and touched the edge of Jesus' robe. "Who touched Me?" Jesus exclaimed. Even though hundreds were touching Him in the crowd, He had felt something when the woman touched Him. Anointing flowed from Him to her. The gift of healing was being displayed. This woman was instantly healed by the operation of this gift.

The gift of healing is a powerful gift of God. This gift operated through Jesus and continued throughout the Book of Acts. Today this precious gift is working. Today the Holy Spirit is passing out the gift of healing. Just as Romans 8:11 declares, in essence, "The same Spirit that raised Jesus from the dead will quicken [make alive] your mortal body," as we draw near to God, this gift will begin to flow out of us to touch a broken and hurting world.

Inspiration Gifts

Prophecy

The gift of prophecy is a powerful gift that is related to several other gifts of the Spirit. It is related to tongues, interpretation of tongues, the word of wisdom, and the word of knowledge. These gifts are similar because they function in relation to what the Bible calls the "spirit of prophecy."

John says the testimony of Jesus is the spirit of prophecy in Revelation 19:10. What he is saying is that prophecy brings us into the realm of the reality of God. Our testimony is our daily experience with Christ. This testimony began when we were first born again. The spirit of prophecy comes upon us and makes the things of God real and alive to us.

When the spirit of prophecy begins to operate, we become aware of spiritual truth. This gift functions with the word of knowledge and the word of wisdom. The Lord begins to speak to us about things that are or things to come. Things that were unclear or unknown become known and sure to us. This gift can be given just for our own edification or can work through us for the edification of others.

King David is a great example of this gift in the Scriptures. The Spirit of the Lord came mightily upon David in First Samuel 16:11. From that time forward David experienced the anointing of the Lord upon his life. One of the strong ways the Spirit operated in David's life was in the gift of prophecy. He began to write prophetic songs that encouraged him, his generation and every generation throughout history.

In Psalm 22, David sang incredibly descriptive words about the crucifixion. In Psalm 110 he sang about the resurrection of Christ and His ministry of heavenly High Priest. In Psalm 27, he sang about the beauty of the manifest presence of God. David sings about drinking in God's presence and spiritual satisfaction in Psalm 63. When you see it you begin to see the incredible prophetic anointing upon David. His words can carry you into that incredible prophetic world.

The gift of tongues with interpretation and prophecy are to edify, exhort, and comfort the Body of Christ.

When you begin to study commentary on the gifts of the Holy Spirit, it is somewhat like reading a comedy. The misinformation from people who aren't baptized with the Holy Spirit is unbelievable. Some will say that prophecy is the gift of preaching, and that whoever is prophesying is a person who has the word of knowledge. I've also read where some believe that when one gets old and has a lot of wisdom, he is known as having the word of wisdom!

Solomon was not necessarily operating in the word of wisdom. He had wisdom from God, which is different. You could be uneducated and receive a word of wisdom through a donkey! Literally! So you do not have to be especially smart or extra spiritual. You must, however, be yielded to God.

Gift of Tongues With Interpretation of Tongues

But one who prophesies speaks to men for edification and exhortation and consolation…. Therefore let one who speaks in a tongue pray that he may interpret (1 Corinthians 14:3,13 NASB).

The vocal gifts operate under the same general laws and rules as the others. Remember, the gift of tongues with interpretation is different from our prayer language where we are speaking to God (see Chapters 3, 4, and 5). The gift of tongues with interpretation is a message from God in a spirit language to the Body of Christ, for the purpose of interpretation. The combination of the gift of tongues with interpretation is equal to the gift of prophecy. Prophecy can be equated to a dime and the gift of tongues and its interpretation can be equated to two nickels. They both equal the same thing.

But there are different ways that God manifests Himself and speaks to the Church. The gift of tongues is an utterance from God in a spirit language for the purpose of interpretation in the church. The gift of tongues with interpretation and prophecy always fulfills these three things: edification, exhortation, and comfort. Edification comes from the word *oikodome*, to build up. Exhortation is the word *paraklesis*, to comfort or help. The word *comfort* comes from the word *paramuthia*, which means consolation. The vocal gifts, then, build up, comfort, or help.

We have taken a look at the nine gifts of the Holy Spirit. These gifts are for every believer. They are not optional, however. In fact, they are necessary for the advancement of the Kingdom. *"Desire earnestly spiritual gifts"* the apostle Paul declared in First Corinthians 14:1 (NASB). Today, we need to pursue and develop these spiritual gifts in the Body of Christ.

Chapter Six

Summary Questions

1. What are the revelation gifts?

2. What are the power gifts?

3. What are the vocal gifts?

4. Who qualifies to use spiritual gifts?

5. What is the difference between our prayer language and the gift of tongues?

CHAPTER SEVEN

The Holy Spirit — The Communicator

For many years, my wife and I traveled to Seoul, Korea, to attend a conference conducted by Dr. Cho. Many times we were accompanied by members of our staff. In 1986, we took several staff members with us and attended the conference, which was partially conducted that year in Osaka, Japan.

One morning we decided to go jogging. However, the street signs in Japan are not written in English, but written with Japanese characters instead. So we took out the English jogging map provided by the hotel. My youth pastor stated confidently, "No problem, I've got this all figured out. Just stay with me. We're not going to have any problems."

Well, he read the map incorrectly and we came out of the park in the opposite direction! That mistake led to many others.

The map showed the directions to go to one spot and take a right, and then go to the next spot and turn left. But we were going farther and farther from our hotel in the wrong direction! We didn't recognize anything. We were lost!

It was our first time in Japan, and we didn't know how we would be accepted there. We had no idea how Americans were thought of by the Japanese. I kept wondering if there may be lingering animosity from World War II. I know there was not, but your mind does strange things when you are far away from home.

We stopped to look at the map one more time. My youth pastor stopped a Japanese man and began to point to the map, trying to communicate with him. But the man couldn't understand him. He just said something in Japanese that seemed to mean "that way." We went this way and that way, here and there. But we stayed lost. As you can imagine, we did a little more running that day than we expected to do!

Finally we found someone who could communicate with us in a few words of English, and we read some of the Japanese names on the signs. He pointed us in the right direction, and we finally found our way back to the hotel.

Not being able to communicate resulted in our becoming lost. Communication is extremely important. It is defined as the vital ability to convey information to others in such a way that the information can be understood. We became lost while jogging in Japan, simply because we were not able to communicate in the language of that culture.

But what is true in the natural world is also true in the spiritual world. If you do not know how to communicate with God, you will become spiritually lost. You will spiritually wander at random, and never find God's clear direction for your life. And since God has chosen to dwell in this age through the person of the Holy Spirit, we must learn how to communicate with Him. As we learn to communicate with the Holy Spirit, we will allow Him to speak to us and direct the course of our lives.

It is important to remember that the communication, lost in the garden when Adam and Eve sinned, was restored after Jesus appeared to His disciples following the resurrection that Easter evening. Another example of restored communication occurred on the day of Pentecost when 120 people were filled with the Holy Spirit and spoke with other tongues as the Spirit of God fell upon them. The day of Pentecost was also a restoration of communication when it reversed what took place at the Tower of Babel. Where confusion and strife once existed at Babel, there was now unity and harmony on the day of Pentecost. Man once again was fellowshipping with God, and man once again was fellowshipping with man.

Jesus came to restore what was lost at the fall of man. He came to live a new relationship with the Holy Spirit. He came to restore a prayer language to our spirit so we can pray and communicate and fellowship with God. He did this through the person of the Holy Spirit. Jesus' ministry lasted for three years. The Holy Spirit's ministry is taking place today on this earth.

The Holy Spirit's ministry began almost 2,000 years ago. We need to learn how to communicate with the Holy Spirit so we can receive all that God has for us.

In Luke chapter 24, we begin with one of four ways in which the Holy Spirit communicates with us to enable us to hear from

God, receive His direction and be used by Him. Luke 24:44-45 takes place after the resurrection as Jesus is speaking to His disciples. He is in His resurrected body, ministering to them shortly after the event in John 20. Jesus said, *"'These are My words which I spoke to you while I was still with you, that all things which are written about Me in the Law of Moses and the Prophets and the Psalms must be fulfilled.' Then He opened their minds to understand the Scriptures"* (Luke 24:44-45 NASB).

Notice what happened. They already had the Old Testament Scriptures. They had Isaiah 53 and Psalm 22, and could read and see the description of Calvary. But their minds were blocked and their eyes were blinded. There were thousands of Jews who did not believe that Jesus was the Messiah. Second Corinthians 4:4 (NASB) states, *"In whose case the god of this world has blinded the minds of the unbelieving so that they might not see the light of the gospel of the glory of Christ, who is the image of God."*

Communication Through the Word of God

One of the ministries of the Holy Spirit is to make the Word of God a living reality in our hearts, applying it directly to our lives. Before I was saved, I determined to read the Bible, beginning in the Book of Genesis. I'd get through two or three chapters and stop. I couldn't understand it because it was foreign to me. It was the most boring book I had ever read. I tried that two or three times.

But when Jesus came into my life and I began to have a relationship with the Holy Spirit, reading the Bible became the most exciting adventure I'd ever experienced. I couldn't get enough of it and had to read it. I devoured it. I realized that the same Spirit who wrote the Book was now living inside of me, and the Bible became revelation to me. The Holy Spirit made the Word of God alive in my heart.

Several years ago my wife and I moved from California to New Orleans to begin our church. We drove in from California with another Christian named Glenn. Glenn was driving the last shift of our trip as I was reading the Bible. The sun was rising early in the morning, and we'd been sleeping as much as we could in the car throughout the night. Just as we were driving into the outskirts of Kenner, Louisiana, I was reading John 4:38 (NASB). It says, *"I sent you to reap that for which you have not labored; others have labored and you have entered into their labor."*

Although I had read this passage of Scripture many times before, the Holy Spirit made it revelation, or *rhema*, to me. I'll never forget when the Lord spoke this into my heart. I knew then that somehow my destiny with God was tied in to a great harvest that was going to take place in New Orleans. I know that this Scripture is just beginning to be fulfilled, and it is going to be fulfilled. It was God's revelation word to me, and it was as if a light turned on inside of me.

When the Word of God becomes "alive" to you as it did for me, this is known as *rhema*. *Rhema* is a Greek word that means "a word spoken for a specific time and place."

It is so important for us to have a lifestyle of prayer and reading God's Word. God will speak to us and give us direction through both. God's Word is not just a book of theology, nor is it a book of rules and regulations, philosophies of men, or a religious book. Our relationship with the Holy Spirit makes the difference between the Bible and the Hindu scriptures, the Koran and all other religious books of the world.

The Holy Spirit of God wrote the Bible. When He lives inside of us, He burns the Scriptures into our hearts to bring direction and revelation to our lives. This is the first way in which the Holy Spirit speaks to us and directs us.

Communication Through God-Given Ideas

First Corinthians 2:9-12 shows us the second way in which the Holy Spirit communicates with us:

> *But just as it is written, "Things which eye has not seen and ear has not heard, and which have not entered the heart of man, all that God has prepared for those who love Him." For to us God revealed them through the Spirit"* (1 Corinthians 2:9-10 NASB).

God reveals His wisdom to us through His Word and through His Spirit. God has revealed these great things that haven't entered into the hearts of men before through His Spirit.

> *...for the Spirit searches all things, even the depths of God. For who among men knows the thoughts of a man except the spirit of the man which is in him? Even so the thoughts of God no one knows except the Spirit of God. Now we have received, not the spirit of the world, but the Spirit who is from God, that we may know the things freely given to us by God* (1 Corinthians 2:10-12 NASB).

God speaks to us and brings us revelation knowledge. Not only does He impart the Word of God, but He puts His own

God-breathed ideas into our minds. His ideas are always ones of success.

One of God's ideas came to me during a time of recreation. God can speak to you during times of recreation if you fellowship with Him by having a prayer life. Several years ago while I was trying to put together the leadership of our church, I saw a great need to minister to the single people of New Orleans. Statistics show there is a large population of unmarried people across America due to divorce, later marriages, and single parenting. That figure is rapidly approaching 40 to 50 percent of the adult population of our country. There is a grave need to minister to these people.

I was praying and seeking God as to how we could minister especially to singles. At that point all of our ministers were previously involved in their own ministries. On this particular day I was doing something very spiritual. I was out on the west course of the City Park Golf Course, walking from the third green to the fourth tee! This thought of how to minister to single people was going over and over in my mind. Right when I walked off of the green, the Holy Spirit gave me a revelation. He began to show me the person He intended to lead this ministry. I had never spoken to this individual about taking this job or any job on our staff but I knew this was the right person for the job. When I made the call, it was a confirmation to this brother of things that the Lord was speaking to Him. The proof of God's wisdom came over the next few years. This ministry began to blossom and for several years was the strongest arm of our church.

If I hadn't been talking with God and communicating with the Holy Spirit, I would have totally missed that revelation and, therefore, would have missed out on a tremendous opportunity to minister to this group of people. We now have numerous home fellowship groups for singles that have developed over the years. That ministry came from an idea given by the Holy Spirit.

Think of the untapped resources for every area. From ministry to the business world, education, etc., it's all open to us because the Spirit of God knows how to grow cotton or tomatoes or whatever your trade is. He knows how to get you in the position to use you for His glory through His ideas, His revelation knowledge.

God wants to speak His plans, His God-breathed ideas, to you for your life. He has a plan marked out just for you that no one else can accomplish.

We need a relationship with the Holy Spirit. He will speak to us, through the Word of God, His ideas for how you can become successful for Him.

Communication Through Spiritual Gifts

In Romans 1:11, we see the third way the Holy Spirit can speak to us. The apostle Paul wrote to the church in Rome before he visited them saying, *"I long to see you so that I may impart some spiritual gift to you, that you may be established"* (Rom. 1:11 NASB). There are gifts of the Holy Spirit that God has given to the Church that bring communication, guidance, revelation, and confirmation into our lives.

There have been two instances in my life where God sent one of His men to bring a "word of confirmation" to my heart.

Before I came to New Orleans, I was attending a Bible school in California. Evangelist and author Dick Mills came to minister at the school. He was ministering and prophesying over the graduates and he gave me a Word from the Lord, using Scriptures. At the time I was confused about several things and had a lack of direction in my life. I had three or four ministerial opportunities and I was all set to make a mistake doing something that was not ordained of God. Dick gave me a list of three or four Scriptures and prayed for me. Three Scriptures that stood out in my mind were: Exodus 14:13, *"Stand still, and see the salvation of the Lord"*; Psalm 2:8 (NKJV), *"Ask of Me, and I will give you the nations for Your inheritance"*; and Psalm 46:10 (NASB), *"Cease striving and know that I am God."*

Striving was a nice word for what I was doing. I was in serious strife! "Be still and know that I am God" was what God was telling me. I also know that the Holy Spirit was telling me to get alone and pray. I did. For the first time in my life I wasn't striving and I asked God to speak His direction for my life and He directed me.

The second time God sent someone to bring a word of confirmation to my heart was when an author/teacher was ministering at our church in New Orleans during what is known as our Harvest Celebration. He spoke to us for one meeting during that week.

We were driving him around the city, and I had been talking to him about the possibility of buying more property. We also discussed the possibility of moving and having new facilities in the future even though the church building we were in at the time had just been expanded. We spoke of nothing specific and the matter was dropped. We were taking him to dinner and as we were driving in the car down Airline Highway, we drove by the property where our new building is now located. I didn't say anything to him about this property, but as we drove by, he looked across the highway and pointed to the property and said, "There's the piece of property you should buy, right there." That was God speaking! Out of all the property we had driven by throughout the day and we weren't even talking about property, and he said, "That is the piece of property you ought to buy to put your church on, right there."

He had no idea that we had already been looking at the land. I thought, "God is speaking to me telling me I am doing what He is telling me to do." I could hear Him speaking to my heart, "I'm confirming My Word to you, son. Obey My voice and I will be your God and cause you to eat the fat of the land."

God confirms His Word. He will bring someone with a word of wisdom, a word of knowledge, or the gift of tongues with interpretation to bring direction and guidance into your life. The Holy Spirit speaks to us in many different ways. Let's not put God in a box. Allow Him to speak to us through His Word, imparted ideas, a man or woman of God, a dream, or one of the gifts of the Holy Spirit.

When He told me to start a church in New Orleans, He spoke to me through a man, the Word of God, a book someone wrote, and a dream. He confirmed it four different ways before I did what He told me to do. God will send His communication to you if you will communicate with the Holy Spirit.

Communication Through Visions and Dreams

"And it shall be in the last days," God says, "that I will pour forth of My Spirit on all mankind; and your sons and

*your daughters shall prophesy, and your young men shall
see visions, and your old men shall dream dreams"* (Acts
2:17 NASB).

Visions and dreams are one of the main ways the Holy Spirit
communicates with us. God has created man in His image. We
are different from the animal creation. We are spirit beings and
have been given a creative imagination that is mandatory for us
to be successful in life.

The Holy Spirit puts His plans clearly in our imagination. As
we pray and seek the Lord, the Holy Spirit will place a picture
in our hearts of our prayers being answered. We will "see" our
unsaved family members lift their hands in surrender to the
Lord. We will "see" our sick bodies totally healed and made
whole. We will "see" our churches filled to capacity and overflowing with new converts. We will "see" with the eyes of our
spirit, the Kingdom of God being established.

Paul taught very clearly about this vital truth. *"While we look
not at the things which are seen* [with the physical eye], *but at the
things which are not seen; for the things which are seen are temporal,
but the things which are not seen are eternal"* (2 Cor. 4:18 NASB).

Paul told us to "fix" our sight on the visions and dreams
given to us by the Holy Spirit. The Holy Spirit will cause you to
rise up strong if you fellowship with Him.

During a Church Growth Conference in 1978, when I first
came into contact with Pastor Cho, I had a small vision in my
heart about what the church was all about. I remember thinking and telling people that if I could get a church of 150 people, I'd be satisfied the rest of my life. That was my idea of
being successful.

My wife and I spent three days in Atlanta at that conference. Karen Hurston, founder of "Small Group Consultation Service," was teaching on visions and dreams. It was at that time that God began to change the picture in my heart of being small-minded about world missions and of being able to touch a city for Jesus Christ. God changed my vision from being small-minded to having His picture of the church: a church reaching the nations for Jesus Christ!

Before this time I had no idea about the possibility of having a great harvest of souls and having a large New Testament church. This concept was foreign to me. The Lord began to speak to me about a great revival before He returns. This was some of the greatest news I had ever heard. This revelation opened me up to God's plans to build a great church in the city of New Orleans.

Communication with the Holy Spirit is very important. He speaks to us through the Word of God, inspired ideas, gifts of the Holy Spirit, and visions and dreams. As we develop an intimate relationship with the Holy Spirit, He will communicate more and more His plans for our lives, our churches, and our communities.

Chapter Seven

Summary Questions

1. How does the Holy Spirit affect our relationship to the Word of God?

2. What role does the Holy Spirit play in making plans?

3. What do spiritual gifts have to do with divine communication?

4. What role do visions and dreams have in divine communication?

CHAPTER EIGHT

Fellowship of the Holy Spirit

One of my favorite verses in the Bible is Second Corinthians 13:24. It is so simple and yet is one of those verses that can be overlooked because it is located at the closing of the letter. This is the way the apostle Paul closed his letter to the church:

The grace of the Lord Jesus Christ, and the love of God, and the fellowship of the Holy Spirit, be with you all (2 Corinthians 13:14 NASB).

Think for a moment about the Trinity revealed throughout Scripture: God, our heavenly Father; His Son, Jesus Christ; and the Holy Spirit. They are all three God. Our Father is God. Jesus, the Son of God in the flesh, and the Holy Spirit, the third person of the Godhead is God. He is God revealed to us.

As we begin to understand God's revelation to us from the Scriptures, we see the role of our heavenly Father and His Person, the Person of Jesus Christ, and the Person of the Holy Spirit. Understanding these three roles changes our relationship with God. Instead of having a nebulous concept of an impersonal God, we begin to relate to Him as a Person. Relating to the Lord personally revolutionizes our prayer life. Again, Second Corinthians 13:14 (NASB) says,

> *The grace of the Lord Jesus Christ, and the love of God, and the fellowship of the Holy Spirit, be with you all.*

In this short verse of revelation Paul gives us a glimpse into the nature of our heavenly Father. He also describes Jesus Christ of Nazareth as well as the Holy Spirit. The first portion of Second Corinthians 13:14 says:

> *The grace of the Lord Jesus Christ...*

"Grace" is Paul's word to describe Jesus Christ. In the Greek, the word for grace is *charis. Charis* is used in our English word *charisma.* Someone who has "pizzazz" in the world is said to have charisma. But the word *charisma* literally means a gift of grace. It is something given to you by God, not because you earned it or because you are special. It wasn't given to you because you are holy, bright, beautiful or rich. You were given this gift of grace simply because God wanted to give it to you.

Jesus comes to this earth and makes prostitutes into holy women of God and pimps into gentlemen. He changes man's nature. Someone who is irresponsible becomes someone responsible. He enters another's life who was once destroyed by poverty, and He brings productivity into that person's life. It is the grace of our Lord Jesus Christ that does that! The grace of our God brings healing and emotional stability and favor. Jesus came to every one of us when our lives were a mess to one degree or another; His *grace* came, not because we deserve it, but because He loves us. Grace is unmerited favor making something that was once ugly into something beautiful. *This* is what Jesus has done!

Second Corinthians 13:14 also tells us that when Paul thinks about his heavenly Father, he thinks of the word "love." John the apostle said three of the most profound words in the Bible, when in First John 4:16, he said, *"God is love."*

God has revealed Himself to us. Everything about the heavenly Father and His creation speaks to us about His wonderful love. When God created man, He created him in His own image. Genesis 1:26 says, *"Let Us make man in Our Image...."* What God was saying was, "Let Us—Father, Son, and Holy Spirit—make man in Our image." God wanted to create man in His image because He was creating someone with whom He could communicate and love.

Just as you want to share life's experience with others, God wants to share *everything* with you. For example, have you ever accomplished anything in a field of sport or in school, and found that no one was there to see your accomplishment? Maybe you just hit your best shot, or ran your best mile, and no one was there with you. It's almost as though it were a waste of time, because no one was there to share your experience. The worst nightmare for a golfer is to hit a hole-in-one when he's playing golf by himself and have no one there to see it! God, in His great majesty and sovereignty, created this awesome universe and He wanted to share it with someone. He wanted to be able to say, "Adam, look at the Grand Canyon! Isn't it beautiful? Isn't that waterfall spectacular? Look at the way the birds fly through the sky, Adam!" Thus, man was created. This reveals God's love.

God also reveals His love in Second Peter 3:9 (NASB):

The Lord is not slow about His promise, as some count slowness, but is patient toward you, not wishing for any to perish but for all to come to repentance.

God is patient and longsuffering. He doesn't want any human being to perish, but rather to come to repentance. God is a holy God and He hates sin. He looks at the murders, the drug rip-offs, the rapes and the violent crimes taking place today, and even though He is deeply grieved with these sins, He is patient. If He wanted to, He could wipe man off the face of the earth. But He is patient because He loves mankind. His goodness and mercy are leading humanity to repentance. God's very creation declares, "I love you!" His longsuffering and patience declares, "I don't want any to suffer eternal damnation. I want all to come to repentance. *I love you.*" But the greatest revelation of our heavenly Father's love was when He looked down at mankind separated from Him because of mankind's sin, and He said, "I love these people so much. I love Adam and Eve and every one of these children, no matter how they have blasphemed, and no matter what grievous sin they have committed. I love them so much that I am going to give My Son, Jesus Christ, to die on their behalf." *That's the revelation of God!*

Paul talked about this in Second Corinthians 9:15 (NASB), when he said, *"Thanks be to God for His indescribable gift!"* Our heavenly Father loves us deeply. He is a God of love, not judgment and condemnation. This is what Paul was saying as he was closing his letter to the Corinthians.

The last portion of Second Corinthians 13:14 (NASB) says:

...and the fellowship of the Holy Spirit, be with you all.

In the Greek, the word for fellowship is *koinonia*. We also see this version of fellowship used in Acts 2:42. When translated, *koinonia*, literally means *fellowship* or *communion*. When you fully understand *koinonia*, your concept about the church, your relationship with the Holy Spirit, and God's Word will change. You will be placed in touch with the God who lives on earth today!

There are three concepts conveyed when referring to the word *koinonia*. The first concept is **fellowship**. Fellowship is intimate friendship. You and I have relationships or friendships with different people. If we are married, our number one friend should be our spouse if we have a wholesome, healthy marriage.

When you enter into fellowship with someone and develop a wonderful relationship, you can begin to understand the relationship it is possible to have with the Holy Spirit. You will see how you can have a wonderful relationship with Someone who loves you.

One aspect of this relationship is simply being able to be yourself. When you are close to someone, for example, you don't have to try to impress that person anymore. Think back to the first time you dated your spouse before you got married. You were on pins and needles! You wanted to make sure your hair was right, your breath smelled right, and your tie was tied right! But as you began to know that person more and more, how you looked didn't matter quite as much. You still wanted to look nice, but he or she had now seen you at your best and at your worst. It didn't matter because of the love between you. This is the way it is when you begin to know God through the person of the Holy Spirit. You don't have to try to impress Him anymore. You know that He loves you just because He loves you and can have fellowship with you.

My wife Parris and I are best friends. We have loved each other deeply for many years, but this love increases as we draw near to God and allow Him to draw us closer to Him. There are no secrets in this relationship. Because of the supernatural nature of this friendship there is perfect trust. We know each has the other's best interests at heart.

Do you have fellowship with someone you trust? Do you have fellowship with the living God? Do you have fellowship with the Holy Spirit? You don't have to hide things from God! He loves you unconditionally. He is our closest, most intimate friend. He wants to bless you and have fellowship with you.

The second concept from the word *koinonia* is **partnership**. This is the word used in the Bible when making reference to the partnership of Peter, James and John in their fishing business. They were linked together. One had a boat, another, a net, and another, business sense. They pooled their resources, catching fish, selling the fish and making money. They prospered and supported their families. That's what a partnership is all about: each member doing his part for the profit of the business or "partnership." The Holy Spirit wants to be our Partner in life. This version of *koinonia* is referring to the partnership of the Holy Spirit.

The Lord is looking for partners to work with to accomplish His plans on the earth. He has chosen to work through human vessels. As Kathryn Kuhlman always said, "He does not need golden vessels; He does not need silver vessels; He only needs yielded vessels."

We are totally dependent on Him to see His work accomplished. We are dependent on His grace, His love, His wisdom, His power, His provision, and His giftings; we need Him for everything. The miracle is that He humbles Himself to work with us. What an incredible honor, to be partners with God. As we enter into this partnership, there are no limitations to what can be accomplished. All things are possible with God.

Partnership is a powerful thing. Recently our city experienced the greatest natural catastrophe in the history of North America. The infrastructure and housing of most of our city was destroyed by Hurricane Katrina in August of 2005. We felt helpless when we returned home to see the devastation of our beautiful city. Words cannot describe the heartbreak we felt as we surveyed the once lively neighborhoods, which were now silent and very empty.

We had no idea of the display of the love of God we were about to see. Ministries from all over the country and even from other nations began to respond. Christian groups and churches began to send resources and volunteers that continued throughout the entire next year. We were surprised and overjoyed at the partnership displayed to our city in this time of crisis. What a display of the love of God! Because of this supernatural partnership, a great harvest of souls has begun in the city of New Orleans.

Another great example of partnership is the special ministry partnership I have with my wife, Parris. Jonathan Edwards spoke of the uncommon union he had with Sarah, his wife. He said the nature of this union was spiritual and he was convinced that it would continue in eternity. Parris and I have fallen in love with Jesus. Because of our common love, a ministry partnership is the result. We are each gifted in different areas. Together, the Holy Spirit displays His glory through this partnership of the Holy Spirit.

This special partnership displayed in marriage is a picture of the life displayed in the partnership of the local church. As we all drink of Him, the walls of separation come down. We begin to experience unity, and the result is a supernatural partnership of ministry. Sounds like revival to me!

God wants to be your partner in every area of your life. Are you in partnership with the Holy Spirit? I'm referring to prayer and worshiping Him every day. "Holy Spirit, I yield my life to You. Do You need a body to work through? Here I am, Lord! This is all I have to give in this partnership, and this I give." And God responds, "Son, all I have I give to you." And He starts pouring into your life. That is partnership with God!

The third concept of *koinonia* is **communication**. One of the Holy Spirit's number one jobs is to communicate with us. Jesus said, "When the Spirit [the Holy Spirit] of Truth comes, He *will testify about Me*" (John 15:26 NASB). The Holy Spirit communicates God's nature to us. The Holy Spirit is the One who drew you and said, "Son, I love you." He pointed you to the cross and said, "Jesus Christ of Nazareth died on this cross for you 2,000 years ago so that you could have eternal life." When we begin to have a relationship with the Holy Spirit, He begins to communicate truth to us from the Word of God. He says, "Look at My Word. My Word is just for you!" Hebrews 13:8 says, "*Jesus*

Christ is the same yesterday, today, and forever!" The Holy Spirit makes the truth alive in our heart and says, "That's right! These promises regarding salvation, health, prosperity and deliverance are for you now!"

I thank God that when I first received Christ there was an instant change in my life. It is not always this way, but it can be if we hear the Word of God and let God work in our lives. I experienced an instant deliverance from certain bondages.

When I look back, I realize that I had heard God's voice. I remember now, hearing, "You've smoked your last cigarette, Frank. You've smoked your last joint and taken your last pill. You've committed your last act of immorality. It's over with…finished. You are set free from that old nature. You've been crucified with Christ. It's finished. That old man is dead." It took two months after that to receive my prayer language and enter into the fullness of the Holy Spirit for my life. But when I was born again, there was an instant work of deliverance. A spiritual revelation of Jesus Christ was imparted into my life and that revelation was, "Jesus is your Deliverer." That meant and still means, "You don't want to smoke anymore. Thank God! You don't have to take drugs or be bound by lust. No longer do you have to be bound by hatred, worry, fear, and strife."

Jesus Christ is the Deliverer. The Holy Spirit comes and communicates this to you and me. Salvation, healing, and deliverance are communicated to us through the Holy Spirit. He also communicates God as our Source and our Provider! The Holy Spirit is the One who brings our marriages together. He heals our broken minds, homes, and families.

Do you need the Holy Spirit to communicate something to you? Do you need Him to communicate that Jesus is your

Healer? Or maybe you need to know Him as the One who baptizes you with His precious Holy Spirit. He fills us with His power so we can worship Him and pray in our prayer language. Do you need to meet Him as your Provider, or as the One who is the Author and Finisher of your faith who will complete what He has begun? Perhaps you need to meet Him as the One who will bring your family back together and make it the beautiful reality that God said it could be. Or perhaps you simply need to meet Him as your Friend who accepts and loves you just as you are.

The Holy Spirit wants to show you love, grace, and fellowship. He wants to enter into partnership with you and communicate with you at all times. He longs for fellowship with you!

Begin today to spend some specific time with the Lord. Worship the name of Jesus, and the Holy Spirit will become very real to you. Let today be the beginning of a whole new relationship between you and the precious Holy Spirit.

Chapter Eight

Summary Questions

1. What does the Greek word *koinonia* mean?

2. How does partnership come into play in our relationship with the Holy Spirit?

3. What role does the Holy Spirit play in fellowship with God?

4. How does the Holy Spirit help us understand the other members of the Godhead?

5. What does *charis* mean?

CHAPTER NINE

Another Helper (Allos Paracletos)

I will ask the Father, and He will give you another Comforter (Counselor, Helper, Intercessor, Advocate, Strengthener, and Standby), that He may remain with you forever — The Spirit of Truth, Whom the world cannot receive (welcome, take to its heart), because it does not see Him or know and recognize Him. But you know and recognize Him, for He lives with you [constantly] and will be in you (John 14:16-17 AMP).

In this Scripture, Jesus was talking to His disciples the night before He went to the cross. At that point, they had not received the Holy Spirit because Jesus had not yet died and risen. Their sins had not yet been washed away. The anointing of God was upon them as they went out and ministered, yet Jesus said there was coming a day when the Holy Spirit was going to be *in* them.

That is the day we live in now, a day that began when Jesus rose from the dead. This day became fulfilled at Pentecost when the Holy Spirit was poured out on the people in the Upper Room and they were filled with the Holy Spirit and spoke with other tongues.

The above verses are from the Amplified Bible. The Amplified Bible takes the Greek New Testament and describes the different meanings in a particular word. Such is the case with the phrase "Another Comforter." There are two Greek words for "another." One of the Greek words, *hetereos*, means "another, but different." It's like saying: Here's a book and here's another book. They are two books yet they are different. Jesus said *"Another Comforter,"* referring to the second definition of another, which is in the Greek, *allos*, meaning "another," but exactly the same as the first. For example, consider two envelopes. Here's one envelope and here's another envelope exactly the same. Jesus said He was sending *"Another"* one just like Himself.

The Holy Spirit is exactly like Jesus. The things Jesus did, the Holy Spirit is doing on earth right now. Jesus opened the eyes of the blind and the ears of the deaf. The Holy Spirit is opening the eyes of the blind and the ears of the deaf today. Jesus proclaimed, "Your sins are forgiven" just as the Holy Spirit proclaims, "Your sins are forgiven" today. The Holy Spirit is just like Jesus, with the exception that He is everywhere at the same time. Jesus was limited on earth because He had a human body, but the Holy Spirit is not limited.

The second word of the phrase "Another Comforter," is known in the Greek as *paraclete* or *paracletos* and can be broken down in several ways. In addition to meaning Comforter, it also means Counselor, Helper, Intercessor, Advocate, Strengthener, and Standby.

In breaking each description down, we see the first one is the **Comforter**. All of us have had a need to be comforted. As I think back, one of earliest memories I have as a child that impacted my life was a funeral I attended.

At the time, I was living in South Carolina and my dad took me on a trip with him to Georgia. That was a big deal for a little boy. All of my relatives lived in the back sticks of Georgia. They made their living in the cotton patch, and my uncle Johnny made cane syrup from his syrup bin. There wasn't a gravel road in town; rather, they were all dirt roads. I was so impressed to be going down those dirt roads with my dad to see our relatives.

When we arrived, I saw the farms and the cotton fields, and I remember Dad telling me about Uncle Johnny's house. That house was 100 years old. We went in, and the wake was in progress. My great uncle, Uncle Cleavy, had died.

There aren't any funeral homes in the back woods of Georgia in this little town, so they had him in the house in an open casket. I thought, "There's a dead body over there, and a casket too!" It was really strange for me to see. Some of the people were pretending as if he wasn't really there; others, however, were very troubled and were grieving.

The next day we went to the funeral service, which was held in a little wooden Pentecostal church, the only church in town. The casket was brought in, and rather than deep grieving, all of a sudden the people began to sing and worship God. Here the casket was being brought in and these people were praising

God. I'll never forget; it was the first time I ever felt God's presence. I was just a little boy, but I saw something. I knew this man wasn't coming back. But the same people I saw crying were also being comforted by the presence of God that was in that place. The Comforter was there! He is real. We have a choice. When you are faced with sorrow or difficult times, you can call out to the Comforter for help.

He's with you right now as you read this. If you are disappointed with life, the Comforter, the Holy Spirit, is there to comfort and lift you up.

Second Corinthians 1:3-4 (NASB) says, *"Blessed be the God and Father of our Lord Jesus Christ, the Father of mercies and God of all comfort, who comforts us in all our affliction so that we will be able to comfort those who are in any affliction with the comfort with which we ourselves are comforted by God."*

The word *paraclete* also means **Counselor**. The best counselor is the Holy Spirit. I have never studied counseling in my life. That may surprise some of you who are familiar with my ministry, but I realize that the only counseling I know and need is that which God tells me. God's Word is my counsel, and the Holy Spirit is my Counselor. When someone comes to me in need of advice, my first response usually is, "Certainly, I'll talk to you, but you know first I'm going to ask you if you've been praying and seeking God and reading your Bible."

A while back we had some relatives staying with us at our home. Often I have my prayer time from nine to ten in the evening. With company, however, it is awkward to do the things you normally do.

I went out a couple of nights when they were there and just walked for my prayer time. I was bringing some challenging problems that I have in ministry before the Lord. I found during those times that I received some of the most supernatural answers from God.

What I would do is set aside 15 minutes and say, "Lord, for the next 15 minutes, I'm going to pray about this specific thing." I would then lift whatever it was before the Lord. I received the best answer to these problems. I could have talked to 10 different people or 100 different people and not have found out what I did from God. He knew exactly what I was supposed to do.

God has a plan for your life, and the only way to find out what it is, is to spend time getting to know Him as a friend. You can say, "Oh, Holy Spirit, You're so precious to me. I need Your direction in my life. Please direct my steps and give me the wisdom of God." James 1:5-8 (NASB) says:

> But if any of you lacks wisdom, let him ask of God, who gives to all men generously and without reproach, and it will be given to him. But he must ask in faith without any doubting, for the one who doubts is like surf of the sea, driven and tossed by the wind. For that man ought not to expect that he will receive anything from the Lord, being a double-minded man, unstable in all his ways.

You do this and He will give you the step-by-step plan for your life.

Jesus said, "It's imperative that I go away!" Man needs this Counselor to come and live inside of him to give him the mind of Christ in his day-to-day life. He's our Counselor.

The definition of *paraclete* continues. The Holy Spirit is also our **Helper**. Romans 8:26-27: *"The Spirit also helps our weakness."* Hebrews 13:5-6 says, *"Let your character be free from the love of money, being content with what you have; for He Himself has said; 'I will never desert you, nor will I ever forsake you,' so that we confidently say, 'The Lord is my helper, I will not be afraid. What shall man do to me?'"* If you have ever had emotional, physical, or spiritual weakness in your life, the Holy Spirit will help you in that area.

Have you ever been tempted to sin before? Perhaps you've been tempted to worry or fear. Maybe you've doubted God, or have wanted to throw it all in and say, "Forget it. It's not worth it." The Holy Spirit helps us in those desperate times of weakness. The Bible says that when we pray in tongues, the Spirit of God prays inside of us and helps us. He joins together with us in prayer.

One of my favorite passages of Scripture is Romans 8:26, which speaks of the Holy Spirit joining together with you against the forces that are coming against you. It reads, *"And in the same way the spirit also helps our weakness; for we do not know how to pray as we should, but the Spirit Himself intercedes for us with groanings too deep for words."*

The Holy Spirit joins with you against sickness, poverty, and financial struggles. Pray in tongues over those areas and the Holy Spirit will join hands with you and help you.

Whatever the situation, picture it complete and pray in tongues over it. Push through into the Spirit realm. Spend 15 minutes, 30 minutes, or an hour praying in tongues, and the Holy Spirit will join together with you and begin to pull against that problem area. The Holy Spirit of God is your solution in every area of your life. He'll work for you.

The definition of *paraclete* also lets us know that the Holy Spirit is our **Intercessor**. Romans 8:26-27 (NASB) says:

> *In the same way the Spirit also helps our weakness; for we do not know how to pray as we should, but the Spirit Himself intercedes for us with groaning too deep for words; and He who searches the hearts knows what the mind of the Spirit is, because He intercedes for the saints according to the will of God.*

If you are ever in a situation where you don't know how or what to pray, pray in the Spirit and the Holy Spirit will direct your prayer. He will actually intercede for and with you, working through your time of prayer.

One night when I was in Coos Bay, Oregon, during my Bible school days, I was sitting in the back of a pickup truck and I and others were coming back from town. We were on our way back to our camp, and I was by myself in the back of the truck. It was probably near 40 degrees outside. Driving along at 50 miles per hour with the wind whipping around, it got very cold.

I began praying, "Oh, God, help! I'm cold!" The spirit of God began to rise up inside of me, and I started praying in tongues. Instead of praying about the cold, I found myself praying for my mom. This was really strange for me because I was a young Christian at the time, and I didn't yet spend lots of time in prayer. But this urgency rose within me, "Pray for your mother…pray for your mother…pray for your mother." I didn't know what was going on, but God was telling me, "Something's happening with your mom. Pray for her."

I found myself almost grieving inside. "Something's wrong," I thought. I just knew it. I prayed for nearly 30 minutes until I felt the need to pray just lift from me.

Shortly after I returned to the camp, I learned that my mom had experienced a stroke. I knew what was happening. Satan was trying to destroy her life. I didn't know all the ins and outs of it, but I know that the Spirit of God told me to pray for her that night and intercede on her behalf.

He knows what, how, and when to pray. He has the answers to what you are going through now and what you are going to face tomorrow. Satan wants to keep us blocked off from the Holy Spirit because the Holy Spirit is the One who leads us in our day-to-day lives. The Holy Spirit will pray through you. He's our Intercessor.

The definition continues, saying that the *paraclete* is our **Advocate**. An advocate is someone who stands up for you. He advocates you, saying, "I'm on your side!"

Sometimes it can seem as if the whole world is against you, or that people are trying to destroy or discourage you. It seems this way especially when you start to launch out in areas of ministry. But remember what David said! *"O Lord, how my adversaries have increased. Many are rising up against me...but Thou, O Lord, art a shield about me, my glory and the one who lifts my head"* (Ps. 3:1,3).

If you're living a godly life in Christ Jesus, you're going to be persecuted by your friends, family, and the devil's crowd. But, thank God, there's Somebody who says, "I'm going to stand with you. I'm your Advocate and I'm on your side. I will work and fight for you, strengthen and be the Strength of your life. I will lift you up and encourage you!" He's our Advocate.

The *paraclete* is also described as our **Strengthener**. I went through something during the spring of 1985 that I had never gone through before in my life. Our leaders' retreat was held in April of that spring, and I was supposed to teach three of four different sessions. When I stood up to teach the first session, however, my mind felt as if it were blank. I stood and tried to teach, but I couldn't even think thoughts or words. I didn't know what was going on. All I would see was a blank picture. It seemed almost as if I was losing my mind.

I sat down, looked at the audience, looked at my Bible, and then back at the audience. I thought, "What's wrong with me?" The devil said, "You're losing your mind." I responded, "Well, it feels like I'm losing my mind!" I thought, "What's going to happen? If I lose my mind, I'll lose my ministry! I can't lose my mind!"

Finally, after we prayed, I began to experience the presence of the Lord. He has not given us a spirit of fear but of love and of power and of sound mind. I felt His strength pouring into me. He is surely the strength of my life.

Have you ever gone through anything like that before? The devil says you're going crazy or you're going to lose your mind. Maybe he's attacked you physically, telling you you're going to lose all your strength or your heart is getting weak. He might tell you your arms and back are getting weak. He might even say you're going to die. *But don't listen to the devil's lies!*

The Holy Spirit will strengthen you if you call on Him and let Him. Remember, the same Spirit that raised Jesus from the dead lives in your body. *"But if the Spirit of Him who raised Jesus from the dead dwells in you, He who raised Christ Jesus from the dead will also give life to your mortal bodies through His Spirit who dwells in you"* (Rom. 8:11 NASB).

Thank God the Holy Spirit is a tangible strength. He was a tangible strength for me when I needed Him at the retreat. He will bring strength to your body and mind. He will quicken your mind through prayer. When you pray, the Holy Spirit will strengthen you. He's our Strengthener!

The last description of the Holy Spirit, the *paraclete*, is our **Standby**. He's always there and won't leave you and take off. He's on standby.

Have you ever traveled standby? It means that you are traveling without a reservation. You wait at the airport and hope someone doesn't show up for his ticket so you can get a seat. You're on standby, waiting for your opportunity to get on board.

There are football players who are the same way. They are not on the first string, but on standby, "standing by," waiting for their chance.

That's who the Holy Spirit is for you. He's on standby, waiting for you when you need Him. He's right there saying, "Let Me in. I'm going to do exactly what you need today. I will be with you, whatever the challenge, and you're going to win. We will go to the top together."

Whether it is a financial, physical, mental, business, family, or spiritual challenge, the Holy Spirit is there! He's our Comforter, Counselor, Helper, Intercessor, Advocate, Strengthener, and Standby. He's our all in all. We desperately need the Holy Spirit in our lives, and He's there for every one of us. He's there for you right now.

Chapter Nine

Summary Questions

1. What does *allos paracletos* mean?

2. In what way is the Holy Spirit…

   a. Our Comforter?

   b. Our Counselor?

   c. Our Helper?

   d. Our Advocate?

   e. Our Standby?

   f. Our Intercessor?

CHAPTER TEN

Jesus and the Holy Spirit: The Purpose of the Anointing

In order for us to grasp the importance of the ministry of the Holy Spirit, we need to look at Him in the life and ministry of Jesus. Jesus Christ was totally dependent upon the Holy Spirit in everything He did. The Holy Spirit was the key to His tremendous impact on the world in His day.

Throughout the years there has been a tendency for man to look at Jesus, His ministry, and the miracles God did through Him with the common misconception that He did these miracles to prove that He was God or the Son of God.

That is a very destructive teaching. Jesus did not perform miracles to prove He was God or the Son of God. As a matter of fact, many times when He would heal someone, He would tell them not to tell anyone.

Jesus did miracles and worked among the people and blessed the people because He was anointed by the Holy Spirit. He gave up His rights as being God. He became a man. He was born a helpless infant in a donkey stable, and then laid in a manger, a feeding trough for animals. He lived a normal life, growing up as a child in Israel, working in His dad's carpentry shop.

Philippians 2:5-11 (NASB) shows us Jesus giving up His rights:

> *Have this attitude in yourselves which was also in Christ Jesus, who, although He existed in the form of God, did not regard equality with God a thing to be grasped, but emptied Himself, taking the form of a bond-servant, and being made in the likeness of men. Being found in appearance as a man, He humbled Himself by becoming obedient to the point of death, even death on a cross. For this reason also, God highly exalted Him, and bestowed on Him the name which is above every name, so that at the name of Jesus **every knee will bow**, of those who are in heaven, and on earth, and under the earth, and that every tongue will confess that Jesus Christ is Lord, to the glory of God the Father.*

This is very important for us to understand. Jesus Himself ministered as a man anointed by the Holy Spirit. This is the same way we minister. He said that we would do the greater works. This is possible as we minister under the anointing, just like Jesus.

But when you realize that Jesus gave up everything in Heaven and became man for 33 years, even though He is God, and ministered as a man anointed by the Holy Spirit, you will also see that this is what gives us hope! This means we can do the things He did.

The same experience Jesus had in the Jordan River is for us today. That experience, being baptized with the Holy Spirit, is what the apostles experienced in the Upper Room. They then began to minister like Jesus, changing from followers to leaders, spectators to participators. Rather than Jesus laying hands on the sick, they were laying hands on the sick. And rather than Jesus casting out devils, they were casting out devils.

Jesus made it very clear that the things He did could be done by His followers, after they received the baptism with the Holy Spirit. John 14:12 (NASB) says, *"Truly, truly, I say to you, he who believes in Me, the works that I do shall he do also; and greater works than these shall he do; because I go to the Father."*

We saw in Philippians 2:4-11 Jesus giving up His rights. He did not, however, give up His deity. He was God in the beginning and He was God as a man. In John chapter 1 we see this truth illustrated. John 1:1 says (NASB), *"In the beginning was the Word, and the Word was with God, and the Word was God."* John 1:14 (NASB) says, *"And the Word became flesh, and dwelt among us, and we beheld His glory, the glory as of the only begotten of the Father, full of grace and truth."*

The word "Word" in these verses refers to Jesus. "In the beginning was Jesus...and Jesus was God" (see John 1:1). He was God when He was raised from the dead and sat down at the right hand of the Father, and He's still God today. He hasn't changed.

But what He actually did for 33 years was give up the privileges that were rightfully His. A *man* had to die on the cross, not an angel or some mystical spiritual being floating around on the earth—a human being, a man, with all the weaknesses you and I face, yet He was without sin.

You must remember that although Jesus became a man, He was still different from all other human beings. He was a man who was not separated from God. He was not born in sin like the rest of humanity. He was born of a virgin, not of the seed of man. The Bible says He was the last Adam. He was as Adam would have been before he fell into sin. Jesus was still in fellowship with the Spirit of God and the Spirit of God was in Him.

For 30 years, though Jesus was God, and the Spirit of God was in Him, He performed no miracles. But as we see in Luke 3:21-22, that was about to change; Jesus' life changed when He received something supernatural from on high.

> *Now it came about when all the people were baptized, that Jesus also was baptized, and while He was praying, heaven was opened, and the Holy Spirit descended upon Him in bodily form like a dove, and a voice came out of heaven saying, Thou are My beloved Son, in Thee I am well-pleased* (Luke 3:21-22).

The Holy Spirit, who was already *inside* of Jesus, now came and rested *upon* Jesus. He was baptized with the Holy Spirit, and something supernatural began in His life. He was anointed by the Holy Spirit, receiving power from on high for a specific task. Notice in Luke 4:14, *"And Jesus returned to Galilee in the power of the Spirit."*

> *And Jesus returned to Galilee in the power of the Spirit; and news about Him spread through all the surrounding district. And He began teaching in their synagogues and was praised by all* (Luke 4:14-15 NASB).

Luke 4:16-19 continues, telling the reasons the Holy Spirit came upon Jesus for ministry!

This was the first time Jesus had read the Scriptures with the Holy Ghost upon Him. He had read the Scriptures as a young man, but something had changed in His life now. He had received power from on high to do the work of the ministry.

> *And He came to Nazareth, where He had been brought up; and as was His custom, He entered the synagogue on the Sabbath, and stood up to read. And the book of the prophet Isaiah was handed to Him. And He opened the book and found the place where it was written, "The Spirit of the Lord is upon Me, because He has anointed Me to preach the Gospel to the poor. He has sent Me to proclaim release to the captives, and recovery of sight to the blind, to set free those who are oppressed* [downtrodden], *to proclaim the favorable year of the Lord"* (Luke 4:16-19 NASB).

We see one of the powerful results of preaching under the anointing as we see what Jesus said about the poor; He said that He came to preach good news to the poor.

The first point to notice here is that our satisfaction in life does not come from the things we own. Our joy comes from our intimate relationship with Christ. Paul spoke about this contentment in Philippians 4:10-12 saying, *"But I rejoiced in the Lord greatly, that now at the last, your care of me hath flourished again; wherein ye were also careful, but ye lacked opportunity. Not that I speak in respect of want: for I have learned, in whatsoever state I am, therewith to be content."* He spoke about a spiritual contentment and joy found in the midst of a lack of abundance.

Second, there is a supernatural provision found for us in the gospel. Jesus displayed this in His miracle of feeding the multitudes. He showed us God's love for us and His willingness to provide for us. Actually, the death of Christ dealt with the root of poverty in our lives. The curse of poverty was carried by Christ on the Cross and the blessing of Abraham comes to us through the power of the gospel. Because of the redemption of Christ, the curse of poverty is broken and we begin to walk in the supernatural provision of the Lord.

For us today, we preach the good news of Jesus Christ. The anointing upon us brings contentment no matter what our circumstances are and also breaks the shackles of poverty from our lives.

The Holy Spirit came upon Him and He was anointed to *set free those who are down trodden* **(see Luke 4:18).**

There are downtrodden people all around you. Maybe you live near a woman in the neighborhood whose husband just left her. She has children to take care of, a house to maintain, bills to pay, a car note, and no training to get a job. There are hundreds of women like this throughout your city right now. You and I have an anointing on our lives to give people hope and help them change. Hope through Jesus Christ is their only way out. We have the answer to heal the downtrodden and lead them into the Kingdom of God.

There are many women in our church who have faced the crisis of no husband and bills to pay, and they have overcome. They haven't had to depend on the Welfare Department of our government nor have they depended on the benevolent department of the church. They learned how to depend on the Holy

Spirit as He directed and equipped them to make a living and support themselves and their families. When circumstances of the world crush you, and you are downtrodden and broken-hearted, nothing else matters except Jesus' love for you. That is the only thing that will meet your need.

There is no crisis too deep that He can't help you through. He will anoint you to go through it and help show you the way out.

He was anointed *"to proclaim release to the captives"* (Luke 4:18).

There were people then as there are today, who are locked and chained to all kinds of sins and habits. Jesus was anointed to proclaim liberty to these people. We read about one of those people closest to Him, Mary Magdalene. She, before having seven demons cast out of her, was bound by sin. But Jesus liberated her.

We see the man let down through the roof to whom Jesus ministered. Jesus looked into his life and He said, *"My son, your sins are forgiven"* (Mark 2:5). This man was a captive not only to the sickness but also to sin. The Word says that Jesus provided liberty to the captives.

I know what it means to be a slave to sin. I received Jesus when I was 21 years old, but the five years before that time, I was miserable. I was a slave of rebellion. I rebelled against my dad, and everything that reeked of authority. I was also in rebellion against God.

In my heart, I recognized that my actions were wrong and weren't pleasing God. There was a part on the inside of me that wanted to do right. When I would do something I wasn't supposed to do, I would hurt on the inside and vow never to do it again. I saw the ugliness of sin. But the next day, I'd be right back repeating what I so deeply hated. In my own willpower, I could not break that power of sin in my life. But through Jesus' power and the power of the Holy Spirit, I could and did!

You cannot break an alcohol or drug addiction problem simply with your own willpower. That's why great organizations that deal with these problems can only take the addict so far. They teach, "once an alcoholic or a drug addict, always an alcoholic or a drug addict." *Thank God that is not true!* I am not an alcoholic or a drug addict because Jesus has given me liberty and anointed me.

He has anointed His people to preach liberty to the captives. If you are born again, you are anointed not only to preach against sin, but to help people get free from sin.

"You are free today from sin, drug addiction and alcohol problems!" That is the message we are to take past the church walls and into the community. The Spirit of the Lord is upon you to proclaim liberty to the captives.

He came to preach *"recovery of sight to the blind"* (Luke 4:18).

The powerful anointing of the Holy Spirit heals the sick of their diseases. Everywhere Jesus went during His earthly ministry the anointing on His life brought tremendous healing to people's bodies.

Even today the power of the Holy Spirit is healing people. One amazing story of God's healing power happened in our church. One Sunday, a homeless man was attending our service. Unknown to anyone at our church, he had a heart condition. He needed heart by-pass surgery. Actually, he was scheduled for an operation at Charity Hospital later that week. This homeless man got in the prayer line at church. That particular day there was a strong anointing of the joy of the Lord in the service. This man found himself under the power of God laughing on the auditorium floor that Sunday. Later that week he went for his prep meetings for his operation and the doctors discovered something amazing. They questioned this man about his heart; they said it was brand-new and needed no operation. They wanted to know what had happened. He told them that he had gone to a church, experienced some unusual intoxication, and found himself on the floor. No one really knows what happened; all we know is that he received a new heart that day.

When Jesus spoke about opening the eyes of the blind, He was also speaking about our spiritual eyes. One of the beautiful things the Holy Spirit does is open the eyes of our heart. Actually, faith is the supernatural ability to perceive things in the spiritual realm. When we come under the influence of the anointing, the things of the unseen world become real to us. The things of God that were uninteresting become not only real, but they become our most valuable possessions.

Finally, **Jesus was anointed to proclaim the favorable year of the Lord.**

This phrase gets to the heart of why Jesus came. He came to restore mankind to intimacy with His heavenly Father. He came to proclaim the year of the favor of the Lord.

Many people preach rules or formulas as a replacement for the gospel message. The message of the gospel is foremost about eternity and about our eternal relationship with Him. It is not an instruction manual or tips on success in life.

The Holy Spirit is actually the atmosphere of a place called Heaven. Have you ever wondered what Heaven will be like? It is a place of amazing love. When we first step into the place called Heaven, we will be amazed at what we experience. Everyone we see will have an incredible look upon their face. Each face will be characterized by a resemblance of Jesus. After all, when we see Him, we will be like Him, changed into His likeness. We will be drawn to the throne of God, the place of incredible joy. As we draw nearer to the throne, we will experience joy unspeakable that will increase in intensity and intimacy throughout all eternity. This joy is actually the joy of the Lord. This is the joy we begin to taste in this life when we are filled with the Spirit.

Some people think of Heaven as a boring place. Floating around on clouds with nothing fun to do. If that is your idea of Heaven, you haven't tasted the reality of God for yourself. When you taste His goodness, Heaven becomes real and you begin to long for its manifestation.

Just as Heaven is a real place, hell is a real place too. Many times we try to ignore its existence, but nevertheless, it is very real. Have you ever thought about eternal suffering? Every person who has ever lived is still alive today. People who lived and died physically are still alive today experiencing the horrors of eternal suffering in hell. Man was created to live forever; the tragedy of the fall of man is that he would be separated from God for eternity. Only through the redemption of Christ can we experience deliverance from eternal hell and enjoy the joys of Heaven for eternity.

The anointing is upon you to proclaim the favor of the Lord. The Lord has provided a place of deliverance from eternal suffering. That place of deliverance is found in the presence of the Lord.

In John 14, we see the relationship with the person of the Holy Spirit that Jesus talked about. The disciples had seen all that Jesus had done and He told them He was leaving. They wondered what it was going to be like when Jesus was gone. "How could anybody possibly replace Jesus?" they thought. "How could we ever do the things that He did? He's the Son of God!" (They struggled with the same concerns you and I struggle with.) But the promise of the anointing of the Holy Spirit that Jesus told them about is here for you and me today!

He gave them a message of encouragement the night before He died. In chapters 14, 15, and 16 of John, He talked with them about the ministry of the Holy Spirit.

> *If you love Me, keep My commandments. And I will ask the Father, ad He will give you Another Helper, that He may be with you forever; that is the Spirit of Truth, whom the world cannot receive, because it does not behold Him or know Him, but you know Him because He abides with you, and will be in you. I will not leave you as orphans; I will come to you. After a little while and the world will behold me no more; but you will behold Me; because I live, you shall live also. In that day you shall know that I am in My Father, and you in Me, and I in you. He who has My commandments and keeps them, he it is who loves Me; and he who loves Me shall be loved by My Father, and I will love him, and will disclose Myself to him (John 14:15-21).*

The Holy Spirit is a Person, and Jesus was referring to the Person of the Holy Spirit when He said "He" may abide in you.

Your marriage, business, health, and attitudes can all change. Negativity can flee. Your whole life can be revitalized through a wonderful relationship with a Person: the Holy Spirit. He wants to do that in our lives!

How can these things be? Can my life really change? Could I possibly experience this anointing within me and upon me?

Absolutely. The anointing of the Holy Spirit is available for all who are thirsty. When you thirst for God, the anointing begins to come. The anointing comes to liberate man by displaying the glory of God. The anointing of the Holy Spirit is actually a Person. He is the awesome third Person of the Trinity. As His glory is poured out, the magnificence of God is clearly seen. As we see and embrace the glory of God, two wonderful things happen: God is glorified and man is satisfied.

We are created by God to enjoy Him forever. Nothing else will satisfy man's hungry heart. When Jesus was on earth, He went to the downtrodden. Their disillusionment with life, because of all of their problems, was obvious. As they came in contact with Christ, they began to be influenced by His anointing. It is the same today. Many times we come to the Lord because of our problems: family, financial, health, and many other things. As we look to Him for our answers, we find an answer bigger than we ever imagined. Not only can He heal, provide for, and restore our relationships, but He unveils Himself to us. We find ourselves lost in His love (see Psalms 16:11).

This is the purpose of the anointing: to unveil the Lord to mankind. As you press into His presence, you will find He is sweeter than honey, He is altogether lovely, He is more than wonderful, and He is all we will ever need.

Chapter Ten

Summary Questions

1. How did Jesus have a miracle ministry?

2. When did Jesus' ministry begin on earth?

3. Jesus preached His first recorded message in Nazareth. What were the five reasons Jesus preached that He had been baptized with the Holy Spirit?

CHAPTER ELEVEN

The Awesome Trinity

The grace of the Lord Jesus Christ, and the love of God, and the communion of the Holy Ghost, be with you all. Amen (2 Corinthians 13:14).

The Trinity is the greatest mystery of all. This awesome God, who is One, has existed in three distinct persons from all eternity. How could there be one God manifesting Himself in three persons? This great truth is a supernatural mystery that we can glimpse through the Scriptures under the inspiration of the Holy Spirit. This great doctrine is hidden and is even foolish to the natural mind, but is precious to the sons and daughters of God.

One of the common titles or references to Jesus in the Scriptures is the Word of God. John refers to Christ as the Word repeatedly in his writing.

In the beginning was the Word, and the Word was with God, and the Word was God (John 1:1).

And the Word was made flesh, and dwelt among us, and we beheld His glory, the glory as of the only begotten of the Father, full of grace and truth (John 1:14).

And I saw heaven opened, and behold a white horse; and He that sat upon him was called Faithful and True, and in righteousness He doth judge and make war. His eyes were as a flame of fire, and on His head were many crowns; and He had a name written, that no man knew, but He Himself. And He was clothed with a vesture dipped in blood: and His name is called The Word of God. And the armies which were in heaven followed Him upon white horses, clothed in fine linen, white and clean (Revelation 19:11-14).

Have you ever thought about what this means? Why does the Word refer to Jesus as "the Word"? Could this hold a key to the understanding of the mystery of the Trinity? I believe it does. The Father displays His glory and His very character and nature in the person of His Son. To understand Jesus as the Word who became flesh is critical to our understanding of God.

What is a word? Actually, a word is the vocal expression of a thought or an idea. This is part of the nature we share as humans. The Lord created us in His image. We have the ability to think of objects or concepts in our mind and express them in a word. A word is a vocalized expression of a thought.

If this is true, how is Jesus the Word of God? Actually Jesus is the manifestation of the Father's thought or idea of Himself. Jesus is the exact representation of the Father. This is why Jesus could say, *"If you have seen Me you have seen the Father"* (John 14:9). That being said, Jesus has always been. He has always been the Word of God. There has never been a time when He did not exist. He is the eternal Word of God, the awesome second person of the Trinity.

> "God's idea of Himself is absolutely perfect and therefore is an express and perfect image of Him, exactly like Him in every respect; there is nothing in the pattern but what is in the representation — substance, life, power nor any thing else, and that in a most absolute perfection of similitude, otherwise it is not a perfect idea. But that which is the express, perfect image of God and in every respect like Him is God to all intents and purposes, because there is nothing wanting: there is nothing in the deity that renders it the deity but what has some thing exactly answering it in this image, which will therefore also render that the deity" (Jonathan Edwards).[1]

Jesus is also referred to in the Book of Hebrews as the radiance or outshining of God.

> *Who being the brightness of His glory and the express image of His person, and upholding all things by the word of His power, when He had by Himself purged our sins, sat down at the right hand of the Majesty on high* (Hebrews 1:3).

He is the display of the beauty and nature of the heavenly Father. One of the awesome facts about this observation of God is that there has never been a time when Jesus was not the radiance of the glory of the Father. There was never a time when this glory was not shining forth. There was never a time when this "light" was turned on or off. He is the eternal radiance of the glory of God, the very image of His nature.

The Father and the Son have existed from eternity. They have an eternal relationship of love from one another. This love is unending, without beginning or end. This is the love that Jesus came to this earth to reveal to us. The love He has enjoyed from eternity is now offered to us.

> *And Jesus, when He was baptized, went up straightway out of the water: and, lo, the heavens were opened unto Him, and He saw the Spirit of God descending like a dove, and lighting upon Him: And lo a voice from heaven, saying, This is My beloved Son, in whom I am well pleased* (Matthew 3:16-17).

> *Then I was by Him, as one brought up with Him: and I was daily His delight, rejoicing always before Him; rejoicing in the habitable part of His earth; and my delights were with the sons of men* (Proverbs 8:30-31).

This love between the Father and the Son is the fellowship that They enjoy and that we have been called into. This is why Jesus came: to display and bring us into the incredible fellowship of love between the Father and the Son.

This mystery of God is far beyond human understanding; it is too good for words. Actually this love between the Father and the Son is supernatural in its nature and is expressed in a distinct Person. The love shared between the Father and the Son is actually a Person, the awesome third Person of the Trinity, the precious Holy Spirit. Jonathan Edwards spoke of this awesome display of God in his *Treatise on Grace*.[2]

"God's love is primarily to Himself, and His infinite delight is in Himself, in the Father and the Son loving and delighting in each other. We often read of the Father loving the Son, and being well pleased in the Son, and the Son loving the Father. In the infinite love and delight that is between these two persons consists the infinite happiness of God. Prov. viii. 30: 'Then I was by him, as one brought up with him: and I was daily his delight, rejoicing always before him'; and therefore seeing the Scripture signifies that the Spirit of God is the love of God, therefore it follows that Holy Spirit proceeds from or is breathed forth from, the Father and the Son in some way or other infinitely above all our conceptions, as the Divine essence entirely flows out and is breathed forth in infinitely pure love and sweet delight from the Father and the Son; and this is that pure river of water of life that proceeds out of the throne of the Father and the Son, as we read at the beginning of the XXIId chapter of the Revelation; for Christ himself tells us that by the water of life, or living water, is meant the Holy Ghost (John vii. 38, 39)."[3]

What an incredible truth, the love of God is so awesome, He is God Himself. God's love is more than an emotion. God's love is actually a demonstration or manifestation of Himself in the third Person of the Trinity.

The Christmas Dance[4]

Before there was history
There lived a great mystery
A story of joy and romance

The Lord and His Son

They've always been One

Embrace in the great Spirit dance

An unspeakable delight

It burst through the night

A joy that's stronger than wine

The Father and Son embracing as

One in the dance that's long

Before time

This singing and dancing

This holy romancing

This joy to the world Angels say

It came to the earth at our dear

Savior's birth

This joy it begins

Christmas Day!

C.S. Lewis spoke about this eternal mystery in his classic book, *Mere Christianity*. He described this relationship as an eternal dance between the Father and the Son. This "dance" is actually a display of the awesome Holy Spirit.

> "That in Christianity God is not a static thing but a dynamic, pulsating activity, a life, almost a kind of drama. Almost, if you will not think me irreverent, a kind of dance. The union between the Father and the Son is such a live concrete thing that this union itself is also a Person. I know this is almost inconceivable, but look at it thus. You know that among human beings,

when they get together in a family, or a club, or a trade union, people talk about the 'spirit' of that family, or club, or trade union. They talk about its 'spirit' because the individual members, when they are together, do really develop particular ways of talking and behaving which they would not have if they were apart.* It is as if a sort of communal personality came into existence. Of course, it is not a real person: it is only rather like a person. But that is just one of the differences between God and us. What grows out of the joint life of the Father and Son is a real Person, is in fact the Third of the three Persons who are God."[5]

The apostle John saw this manifestation of the Trinity and wrote about it in Revelation 22:1.

And he shewed me a pure river of water of life, clear as crystal, proceeding out of the throne of God and of the Lamb (Revelation 22:1).

This river is the Holy Spirit and He is constantly proceeding from the Father and the Son. The river is not just an experience; it is a person. The river is the precious Holy Spirit who has always proceeded from the Father and the Son.

Today the Holy Spirit is flowing like a river from the throne of God. He is falling on every tribe and every tongue. He is gathering His children together from every corner of the earth. Today, His presence is calling out to you and to me. He is saying: "Come to Me and drink, all who are thirsty. Come and drink and be satisfied in the depths of your soul."

And the Spirit and the bride say, Come. And let him that heareth say, Come. And let him that is athirst come. And whosoever will, let him take the water of life freely (Revelation 22:17).

All throughout the earth today, man's heart is crying out. Restlessness is calling out to rest, thirst is calling out for drink, hunger is crying out for nourishment. Man is wandering in darkness longing to see the light found only in Christ. If you are thirsty, call upon the name of the Lord. He will surely hear your cry and come to you in the person of the Holy Spirit.

Even so, come, Lord Jesus (Revelation 22:20).

Chapter Eleven

Summary Questions

1. What do the Scriptures mean when they refer to Jesus as the Word of God?

2. When did the Word of God come into existence?

3. Who is the object of the Father's love?

4. How is this relationship between the Father and the Son related to the Holy Spirit?

5. In light of the teaching of this chapter, why did Jesus come to earth?

Endnotes

1. Lee, Sang Hyun, ed. *The Works of Jonathan Edwards Series Volume 21: Writings on the Trinity, Grace and Father* (New Haven, CT: Yale University Press, 2003) 114.

2. Lee, Sang Hyun, ed. *The Works of Jonathan Edwards Series Volume 21: Writings on the Trinity, Grace, and Father* (New Haven, CT: Yale University Press, 2003) 184.

3. Jonathan Edwards. *Treatise on Grace & Other Posthumously Published Writings Including Observations on the Trinity.* (Cambridge: James Clarke & Co. Ltd., 1971) 101.

4. Frank Bailey. "The Christmas Dance." (New Orleans, Louisiana: Carpenter's Publishing, 2005).

5. C.S. Lewis. *Mere Christianity.* (Hammersmith, London: HarperCollins Publishers, 2001) 175.

Ministry Contact Information

Victory Fellowship
5708 Airline Dr.
Metairie, LA 70003

Church Office Telephone: 504-733-5005
Fax: 504-733-1939
Victory Christian Academy: 504-733-5087

E-mail: info@victoryfellowship.net
Website: http://www.victoryfellowship.net

Also available from Victory Fellowship and Frank Bailey

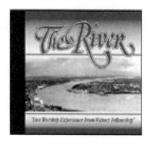

The River

On and On...

Elevator Music

Call toll free in the USA or log on to order:

1-888-733-5077

www.victoryfellowship.net

Additional copies of this book and other
book titles from DESTINY IMAGE are
available at your local bookstore.

Call toll-free: 1-800-722-6774.

Send a request for a catalog to:

Destiny Image® Publishers, Inc.
P.O. Box 310
Shippensburg, PA 17257-0310

*"Speaking to the Purposes of God for this
Generation and for the Generations to Come."*

**For a complete list of our titles,
visit us at www.destinyimage.com.**